Far North Tales
an Alaskan Anthology

By Avril Johannes

Published by
ICICLE FALLS PUBLISHING
HC 31 BOX 5118A
WASILLA
ALASKA 99654
Avril.j@gci.net

Far North Tales
an Alaskan Anthology

BY
AVRIL JOHANNES

COVER PHOTOGRAPH: AVRIL JOHANNES

COVER DESIGN: MARK JOHANNES

PUBLISHED BY
ICICLE FALLS PUBLISHING
HC 31 BOX 5118A
WASILLA
ALASKA 99654

ISBN 9780-9749360-4-8

Available through:
Todd Communications
203 W. 15th Ave. Suite 102
Anchorage, AK 99501
(907) 274-8633
Fax (907) 276-6858
WWW.ALASKABOOKSANDCALENDARS.COM

Other books by Avril Johannes
When The Wolf Calls.

Co-authored with Jan Branham
Squeak An Alaskan Squirrel.
Eeny, Meeny, Miney, Moe Four Alaskan Ravens.
Bunny An Alaskan Hare.

DEDICATION

For Joe, who made it all possible.

To

AARON

Best wishes

[signature]

TABLE OF CONTENTS

Roots and Wings..07
Bunny From The Baskerville.................................10
Cast Iron Cookware and a Broken Promise 13
Bats 17
Cody Cat..18
Family Bush Life..21
Iditarod 2003 24
The Whisper Of Snowflakes 29
Faeries And Their Ilk..33
Goldie Horse 37
A Bush Christmas 39
My Halibut Fishing Trip..45
Snowmen 50
Dear World 52
Cabin Fever...54
Our Wilderness Home...57
Away From The City 61
A Different Kind Of Hobby 65
Restless Spirits...69
The Predator 72
Radiosonde 76
The Goshawk I wanted To Kill 81
Puff...84
A Moose Hunt..86
The Gyrfalcon 92
The Land Remembers 94
Wiley Coyote 95
Hatcher Pass 97
Blem Scoter...101
Kodiak 104
Our First Wild Patient 110

Cataclysm..114

The Dump And Other Fun Places 118

The Voices Of Bonanza Creek 121

Delta Buffalo 126

Raising Ravens 130

Squeak...134

The Hawk That Stole My Heart................................137

Trip To Southeast 145

Mosquitoes...150

Our Daughter's Wedding.......................................152

A Nightmare 154

George...155

Paddles..159

A New Life In Oregon 161

Backyard Battle...164

Sleepy Companions 167

My Black Swans 170

Home Again 173

ROOTS AND WINGS

The pilot's voice interrupted my reverie. "You want to take the controls?" he asked.

Shocked at his offer, all I could do was nod: I'd never flown a plane before. The Cessna 172's responsiveness to my touch, the sense of power and the freedom were exhilarating.

"What a rush," I said as he took over a few moments later.

Relaxed and free from earthly bounds, my mind wandered back to what I call "The Summer of Flight." That was when our eldest son, Mark, a teen still yet to shave for the first time, left home to learn to fly. And I, badly missing him, suddenly found myself the surrogate mother of a scrawny baby red-tailed hawk.

Mark had talked about wanting to fly for years. I argued against it. "You're only 15," I said. "The time's not right. Wait till you're older. At least get your driver's license first."

"Come on, Mom," he replied. "I can learn to drive any time. I want to fly now."

I had a mother's fears. Even though he'd stay with people we trusted, I worried he was too young to risk such adult things. He was my first-born. I'd dried his tears, tended his wounds. What if the plane crashed? Besides, he'd be 350 miles away in Anchorage, a city with many temptations, and he'd only come home occasionally. Finally, persuaded, I agreed. As he was leaving, my father's favorite saying swept soulfully through my mind: "The greatest gifts you can give your children are roots and wings."

Mark was home for a weekend in June when the local Game Warden called. "Have some baby hawks for you. They're young, one really young. You'll have them for a while," he said. We held the necessary permits.

Late Sunday, Mark and Joe talked about flying. Joe had flown small planes for years, but finances dictated he give it up. They joked about their first landing and touch-and-go. "Yeah," I heard Mark say. "I bounced a couple of times, but the instructor told me, 'You'll catch on.'"

"Were you scared?" I asked.

"Not really," he answered.

But I felt anxious. Like a mother hen, I loved having all my brood safely tucked under my wing. Mark returned to Anchorage the following day. I'd miss him.

A week after he left, a huge storm blew through our valley. Mark called that evening. The first words out of my mouth were, "Did it storm in Anchorage?"

"It was a beaut!" he laughed. "Lots of lightning and thunder." Then, as if reading my mind, he added, "No, Mom, I wasn't even at the airport."

My heart eased back into place. I should have known he wouldn't take chances. He said, "I'm working hard on Ground School, and hope to have my license before summer's end."

"I'm proud of you, Mark," I said before hanging up.

Ten days passed before he called again. He asked what I'd been doing. I told him, "I was trying to get the baby hawk ready to solo, but she seems to be fighting it."

"Give her time, Mom," he said. "She'll do it when she's ready."

Just as life seemed to be gliding along nicely, my world fell apart. Calling from England, my brother told me my father had unexpectedly slipped into a coma. I should come immediately. Joe and I hurried to the airport in Anchorage so I could catch an over-the-pole flight. After my arrival at my dad's bedside, I barely had time to whisper, "I love you," before he shook loose his earthly roots. "He waited for you," the doctors told me. My heart hurt at the thought he'd no longer be there.

I returned to my family ten days later. Knowing how close I'd been to my dad, Mark came home to help me through my loss. Edgy, weepy and out of synch, I needed to get back into the routine of our lives, keep busy. I'd concentrate on the baby hawk--that would help. She'd missed her flying lessons while I'd been away.

In mid September we released her. Mark was home again. She was ready to go. As we watched her until she disappeared into the cloudless blue sky, Mark said, "I told you she'd fly when she was ready, Mom". Standing there, I felt like part of me went with her. She'd helped me through the very tough time of losing my father.

The next morning Mark returned to Anchorage to finish flight school. Two weeks later he called to tell us he'd flown solo for the first time. "I did it," he hollered. "It was great."

Mark, like the young hawk, had worked hard to gain independence and the freedom to soar. Joe and I were thrilled.

Jarring me loose from my daydreaming, the pilot suddenly banked the plane to the right. Pointing to sunlight glistening on glacial blue ice below he said, "Look down there."

How competent he seemed, how secure in himself and his abilities. I felt safe.

"What're you thinking about, Mom?" he asked, his voice crackling in my headset.

"Oh, your grandpa's favorite saying about roots and wings, and how extremely proud I am of you. Your father and I gave you your roots, Mark. You earned your wings," I said.

THE BUNNY FROM THE BASKERVILLE

Friends visiting our farm outside of Fairbanks often referred to it as, "The Watering Hole", or "The Haven," for our domestic critters, and injured wildlife of the area. We were asked on several occasion why the members of our, "Other Family" got along so well. After all, as people pointed out, we had prey and predator together in a confined area.

We explained that wild animals do live in harmony in nature until hunger drives a predator to kill. It is common knowledge wolves roam among caribou herds without causing alarm, and lions in Africa mingle compatibly with zebra and gazelle during times when need for food is not a priority. All we needed to do was keep those in our care well fed.

Rajjet, a Chocolate Dutch rabbit considered prey not predator, arrived Easter morning. He was a small, furry gift for our daughter. Sitting quietly among brightly colored eggs and candy he looked like such a precious, harmless ball of fuzz.

The family loved, cuddled and pampered him from the moment he arrived. He followed us everywhere, both inside and out. His day began with being let out of his cage, and a loving session from whoever could get to him first.

He spent his days outside in the yard, fields or nearby woods, and came hopping to the house at night when called. We felt he would be safer in the house during nighttime hours. Several predators lived in our area and we feared he might become a midnight snack for a fox, wolf, owl or lynx. Instead of worrying about him, we should have feared for their well-being.

Rajjet's disposition changed slowly. We were unaware of his tyrannical ways until they were fully established. It all started with his chewing things in the house; chair legs, lower cabinet doors, books and magazines. Then he graduated to harassing Puff, our daughter's poodle. Whenever he was within striking range during the day, he nipped the dog on the nose often causing it to bleed. From that he progressed to aggravating Puff at night. While Puff slept, Rajjet bounded at full speed right over the top of him then, as soon as Puff settled back to rest, he struck again. This all took place in our bedroom while we were trying to sleep.

One evening Rajjet failed to come when called. Flashlight in hand I walked the fields searching for him. After finally giving up I returned to the house and spent the night worrying about him. At daybreak I found him on the lawn, dragging his broken leg behind him. He'd managed to get home.

Confined to a large cage until his splinted leg healed, he was a subdued bunny. However, once the splint was removed he soon became his old obnoxious self, terrorizing Puff at every opportunity.

In the house, he and the three Snowshoe Hares we were raising to maturity, chased, boxed, played tag, and jumped over each other. The four cleaned one another, shared their food, snuggled up and slept together. We thought the reason Rajjet got along with them was because we never handled the hares. We didn't want to remove their fear of man; they were to be returned to the wilds when they matured.

During the days, both Puff and Rajjet spent time outside. The rabbit followed the poodle everywhere. At first we thought they were playing when they chased each other across the grass. Soon we realized this was not a game. Rajjet tearing along behind Puff nipped him in the rear and bit his hind legs, coming away with a mouthful of curly hair. When Puff stopped and turned, Rajjet positioned himself directly in front of his face. Puff waited for the eminent attack. When it failed to materialize he stretched his head forward attempting to lick Rajjet. It was then that Rajjet sprung into action, biting Puff's tongue, which caused profuse bleeding, yelping, and general mayhem.

We resorted to putting the dog in and the rabbit out, or vice versa. Inside, Rajjet behaved part of the time. Outside he was a full-time tyrant. One day he decided to eat on the same pile of hay Mabel, our children's pony, was munching on. The good-natured pony, a gentle sort, allowed this without objection. Peace reigned until Rajjet decided he wanted the hay Mabel had in her mouth. He rose up on his back legs and bit her on the lip. She struck out with her front hoof. Luckily, she missed.

Rajjet attacked Missy Goose as she sped away honking and flapping her wings while he, with a mouthful of feathers, sat on his haunches calmly watching.

He chased the chickens, turkeys, ducks, geese, and peafowl. The only birds he left alone were our pheasants and quail. He couldn't get into their pens!

For all Rajjet's hateful ways, he was a loving little creature at times. He jumped onto our lap waiting to be petted, wanting to be loved. He enjoyed having the top of his nose scratched, pushing his little brown head under our hands to show his pleasure. In the evenings, he sprawled on a mat next to Puff in front of the fire. Then, in one fluid movement he flipped himself over. Lying flat on his stomach like a dog, he stretched out his front legs, and his hind legs straight out behind him. Not the usual way for a rabbit to relax.

When my husband brought a Husky puppy home for me, unlike Puff, Smokey retaliated when Rajjet attempted to bite him. It was obvious Rajjet was not going to change his ways, and we didn't want to cage him after allowing him freedom. He was exiled to the barn for his safety, and our peace of mind.

He loved the barn and all its inhabitants. He sat on Mabel's shaggy back, ate with the chickens and turkeys, and finally fell in love with a Bantam hen. He followed her everywhere. He nuzzled her, and in return at night she covered him with one wing. Watching them, it was not hard to see where the myth about the Easter Bunny Egg originated.

CAST IRON COOKWARE AND A BROKEN PROMISE

I grew up in an old farmhouse without electricity, in England. My mother cooked on a woodstove that also heated our home. We hand-pumped water from the well into a holding tank up on the roof, which then gravity fed to the kitchen and bathroom. After dark we read and worked by the light of oil filled Aladdin lamps. I promised myself that once I left home I'd never live that way again. Every modern convenience would be mine.

As a child, I didn't realize what it must have been like for my mother to jump out of a nice warm bed, shiver her way to the kitchen, and stoke a fire before the rest of her family stirred. By the time I struggled to my feet the house was warmed and breakfast was waiting.

The years passed, I graduated from school and joined the work force. With my job over for the day, I rushed home to my small, thatched cottage, switched on the light, turned up the furnace, and cooked a meal on my electric stove. Before retiring for the night, I climbed into a hot scented bath and relaxed with a good book. It was pure unadulterated luxury.

Little did I realize then that life would move me to Fairbanks, Alaska, or that my husband and I would search for a home in the woods. With three children to raise, and town life not fitting what we wanted for them, we decided to move to the country. Already a close-knit family, we planned to home-school our children, live off the land to the degree that is possible in Alaska. We hunted, fished, raised poultry for meat and eggs, and goats for milk.

For a year we searched for a remote piece of property. Then, by a chance, we found just the right place: ten acres in the middle of nowhere, a large, old log house, his and her outhouse, several log cabins, and mountains surrounding the valley. Situated miles from the closest town, we had no power and no running water, but we did have a wood cook stove, a barrel stove in the living room, and several oil lamps lined up on a shelf. Suddenly I was back to my childhood, my promise to myself long forgotten. Now I appreciated those years of experience on my parent's farm.

My cook stove differed from the one my mother used in England. Hers, as well as having a built-in tank containing hot water any time a fire burned, also heated their home with water circulating through copper pipes surrounding the inside walls. Besides the cooking oven it had two warming ovens, which were used for all manner of things: they often housed rows of newly born puppies, and piglets mothers refused to nurse, and cardboard boxes of baby chicks, turkey poults, ducklings and goslings. My parents designated me to take care of them. I loved it.

With a casualness that deceived me, my mother cooked everything to perfection in the main oven. At the far right of the stovetop, away from the firebox, I watched her make cottage cheese and cream cheese. She also kept a five-gallon pan of milk warm on that section of the stove to bottle-feed baby animals.

As I struggled to learn how to use my wood cook stove, my mother came to mind every day. How easy she'd made it appear to light the fire, keep it stoked, and create the right temperature for pies, bread, and roasts. My poor family suffered through many disasters of burnt offerings, and overcooked or underdone meals before I understood the art of regulating the heat. And, those times I placed a box of baby chicks in the warming oven, I offered up many anxious prayers.

All my cooking utensils were cast iron, the care of which turned out to be another thing I should have paid closer attention to when my mother said, "Remember this," as she explained how to make them non-stick. Finally, in desperation, after destroying eggs while trying to fry them Sunnyside up, I mailed a panicky letter to seek her advice. Through her reply I did figure it out. It wasn't complicated, but definitely necessary in order to not have everything stick to the bottom and sides of my pans.

This is the letter I received from her. Now that you've already scratched your cookware, you'll have to start all over with the things you should have done - before using them. If you do what I tell you, you'll have non-stick pans for life. DON'T ever scrub them once you've done what I tell you. And remember, the blacker they look, the better they work.

First wash pans in hot soapy water then use coarse steel wool to scrub the entire coating from the bottom – inside and out. Wash again, rinse well and dry. Then rub the entire surface with a generous coating of suet. Place pans in 425-degree oven – or as close to it as you can get, for fifteen minutes. Remove, cool, then lightly recoat only the inside with suet. Return to oven for another fifteen minutes. Remove and cool again, then smear a HEAVY coat of suet on the inside. Place pan back in oven for two hours. Let oven cool down and leave the pan in there until the next day. Wash in hot soapy water, rinse and dry. That, my dear child, should take care of your problem.

It worked for my frying pans, and Dutch oven that I loved for its capability of fixing complete meals, and the Gem pan (Muffin,) and griddle that I ended up leaving for the people who bought our property when we moved away. I kept my frying pans. One of them I'm still using on my electric stove some thirty years later. The other I gave to my daughter, who had previously thought them ugly. However, after years of using and scratching so called non-stick cookware, she now loves her cast iron pan.

Making muffins in a cast iron pan was different from using paper Bake Cups. I greased my Gem pan then placed it into the hot woodstove oven. While it heated, I sifted 1-cup flour and 2 teaspoons baking powder into a bowl. In another bowl I broke an egg, beat it, added 1-teaspoon sugar, a pinch of salt, and some melted butter. Then added the flour mixture and a 1/2-cup milk to it. By the time I finished, the pan was smoking hot and ready for the batter. I baked the muffins for approximately 10 minutes.

The thing that's nice about this recipe is that anything can be added to it. Cranberries, Blueberries, or Raisins, plus, it can easily be doubled or tripled.

Muffins made a handy snack for my family. Our boys especially enjoyed them hot out of the oven, slathered with butter and homemade jelly when they returned from wood-cutting – a chore that required numerous trips and strenuous labor. Our long, hard, Interior winters required cords of felled and chopped wood to heat our house, and keep the cook stove burning all year.

Our sons worked hard, but made the most of their time in the woods. They never failed to come home with stories of things they'd discovered: discarded moose antlers, an eagle nest, a deserted den, fossils, petrified wood, ideal places for them to set traps, and sheep on the mountain.

Looking back, I must say, "Our time in the Bush was the most content I've ever been," and for someone who promised they'd never again live without electricity and running water, I can't imagine my life without those incredible years.

BATS

Temperatures below zero meant little or nothing to us most of the winter. As Joe used to tell people, "We just chuck another log on the fire." We were warm and safe inside our house, with plenty of food, and firewood gathered during the summer and fall. We collected water from a nearby river, which never froze. It flowed continuously year around, but once the water was removed from the river in winter it froze solid. We thought it might have something to do with the mineral content. The times we decided it was too cold to fetch water, we melted a bucket of snow on our barrel stove.

Wintertime held special moments that had little to do with survival. It gave us time to sit around the kitchen table and talk about anything that came to mind. Time the whole family enjoyed.

One evening our conversation caused anxious moments for Mark, our oldest son, and lots of laughs for the rest of us. Except for Mark, we had all seen bats flying around the house, cabins, outhouse and barn, but Mark was convinced that if there were any bats, they were confined to our belfries. When we tried to show them to him, they were gone by the time he ran outside.

One evening our daughter sat contentedly flipping through a magazine. She came across an article about bats. The story said bats hibernate during the cold months. This brought up the discussion of where they might do that in our particular part of the world. Several places came to our mind: cabins and house eaves, inside the barn, the hen house and last, but still a possibility, under the seats in the outhouse. From then on, sitting in the dimly moonlit privy contemplating life and the habits of bats held a whole new meaning for Mark. Slightly unnerved, he moved a little faster.

CODY CAT

Cody and I lived together for seventeen years, almost as long as with my children before they graduated and left home. Like them, she was the reason behind many memorable times.

I found her as a tiny kitten with eyes still cloudy- blue; too young to survive on her own. I bottle-fed her until she learned to lap from a saucer. From then on she grew in size, independence, and self-assurance.

Cody learned to be proficient hunting mice, birds, moles, and gophers, but still loudly demanded her food dish be filled each morning. At night she slept on my bed until dawn then, licking the end of my nose until I awoke and crawled out of bed, she marched to the door and insisted I let her out.

When she was two, I opened the door late one morning to let her back into the house and found her on the porch with her intestines lying beside her, and her back leg barely hanging on by a small piece of skin. Placing her tenderly in a box, I rushed to the veterinarian, expecting him to put her to sleep. On the way, I promised her, "I'll stay with you 'till the end, little girl."

After examining Cody, the veterinarian said, "From the looks of her, she's been in a fight, probably with a raccoon. I might be able to put her back together. Want me to try?" Excited, I drove home and waited for a call telling me when to pick her up.

She was a pathetic sight with most of her hair removed, rows and rows of stitches surrounded by Betadine painted skin after her surgery. We left the clinic late in that afternoon.

She required care and attention. Tiny, piteous mewing brought me to her side immediately. As I sat petting her head, I told her, "You're a lucky girl, you know that? I hope you realize you've already used up one of your lives." Two weeks later, she climbed an apple tree outside my bedroom window and stayed there all afternoon lounging in the sun.

Her next misadventure happened on one of her hunting

forays. My neighbor had set out strychnine to dispense with moles and ground squirrels. Cody managed to catch and eat one already poisoned. Back to the veterinarian once more. This time he didn't hold out much hope. He medicated her, and said, "Take her home." My promise to stay with her crept into my mind.

Once again, I played nursemaid. A week later Cody wanted to go out. Reluctant, I reminded her, "Don't forget you only have seven lives left, young lady." She looked at me, stuck her head in the air and scampered outside.

For the next three years her life was uneventful. Then she needed bladder surgery, which caused her a great amount of pain. I kept telling her, "You're a tough little girl. You'll be fine." She was. She healed well and no problems surfaced.

The day I moved back to Alaska, having made all the necessary arrangements for her and Missy, my dog, to travel with me, she sped out the door and hid under the house. Regardless of how I tempted her, she refused to come out. With friends promising to send her to me as soon as they caught her, I left. It took them two months before they finally cornered her.

Their call announcing her arrival sent me racing to the Anchorage airport. As soon as Cody heard my voice, she responded with a loud meow. She was skinny, scruffy and dirty. I hardly recognized her. Later, I found out she had survived off the land the entire time. She had refused to come to anybody to be fed.

In the car, I let her out of her carrier. She licked Missy's face then climbed onto my shoulders for the trip home. Inside the house, she checked out the furniture, the rooms, and my bed where she slept at night. After satisfying her curiosity, she demanded food and undivided attention. Happy to have her back I didn't object. After she settled in, she lost much of her independence, spending her time close to me.

Then one day in the following spring, while I was in town, she walked under the arm of my kitchen faucet. I came home to a completely flooded house. For a moment I was tempted to drown her in the mess she'd created.

That fall, while having my electric heating system converted to natural gas, Cody caused me to do damage to the house. In her haste to find a safe place to hide from the workmen, she scrambled through a hole they had cut to run pipe from one room to another. Nobody noticed.

Sometime during the night I heard her calling. I searched the house, looked outside, but was unable to locate her. About three o'clock in the morning I climbed out of bed to use the bathroom. Again, I heard a hollow sounding meow. I called her. She answered but didn't come. After several tries to locate her, it finally dawned on me; she was behind the wall. I called my son to ask, "How do I get her out?" A moment of silence, then, "Mother, get a hammer and break a small hole in the sheetrock, just big enough for her to get through. She'll come out."

In the hour I sat trying to persuade her to come to me, she retreated further back inside the wall. I panicked, and ended up smashing a gap large enough for me to crawl through. I grabbed her, hauled her into the room, stuffed a pillow in the hole, then released her. Purring all the while, she wrapped herself around my legs.

Later, when she jumped up on the bed to spend what remained of the night with me, I said, "One of these days you're going to run out of lives, old girl." She curled up next to my pillow. That was her last escapade.

At age seventeen, she stopped eating. I knew her time with me was running out. As she grew weaker, she stayed with me constantly. Once again, holding her, I told her, "Don't worry, I'll stay with you, Cody."

On her last day, she refused to eat or drink. I devoted all my time to her. That night, she died. She came to my bed, meowed once, as if to say goodbye, then lay down next to me. I placed my hand on her side as she drew her last breath. I'd kept my promise.

I buried Cody in her favorite spot, the place she loved to sleep in the sun's warmth.

Several nights later, I stood outside looking at the sky and thinking of her. Stars twinkled and constellations shined brightly. Standing there, I envisioned Cody stalking Celestial mice, with Orion the hunter as her guide.

FAMILY BUSH LIFE

A summer-long project for our boys, the winter wood supply was not new to them. They had supplied wood for our fireplace in Fairbanks, but now in a remote area, with no other means to supplement heat or ability to cook, it required many more cords of logs; we figured approximately fifteen to twenty cords.

The average snowfall, a hundred and forty-four inches for our area, meant hard work for the boys. However, they enjoyed the time spent in the woods. They hooked up sleds behind snowmachines to haul home eight-foot tree lengths, then cut them into stove size pieces. To keep those dry and out of the weather, the whole family stacked them in a shelter Joe and our boys built.

In the evenings, sitting in the comfort of a warm house, the boys told us about the animal tracks they'd seen during their days in the woods: marten under a tree, mink down by the river, coyote that ended abruptly by a pile of feathers, porcupine in a creek bed, as well as cloven hoofed moose tracks. They checked out ermine prints following mouse indentations, as well as porcupine-chewed antlers. Though the work was strenuous, the boys managed to mix pleasure with their task.

Joe and I thought our children needed time alone to be themselves, and we believed the country was the place for them to do it. It gave them an opportunity to properly evaluate themselves and their surroundings. We wanted them to understand there's a place for everything and everybody, but it was up them to make decisions for themselves, and realize their choices might make a difference in Nature's balance.

Living as we did, we were our children's greatest influence. Their formal education was Home Correspondence. An Advisory teacher in Juneau helped us when we needed it. At times, our daughter missed the friends she'd had since first grade. However, being busy with work or play helped those moments pass. Some of our friends thought we deprived our children of, "The finer things in life," as they said. We disagreed. What we felt were the finer things in life might never be available to them again, except on vacation or a weekend trip to the country once they left home.

One thing we thought advantageous was jumping out of bed in the morning, looking out the window at a valley that ended at the foot of a spectacular 5,975-foot mountain called Meikle. We studied that mountain through spotting scopes, searched with binoculars to see any wildlife on the move, and spied on the resident eagles nesting below timberline. We watched the moon rise behind its peak, and enjoyed sunsets that left it framed in a sky streaked with deep orange, blood red, and brilliant yellow.

In hunting season we searched the valley for moose, the ridges for sheep. Hunting season would be different for us in these new surroundings. In the Fairbanks area, the only large animal Joe and the boys hunted was moose. Now there were Dall sheep and Caribou. Mark and Scott shot their first full-curl Dall rams on ridges in Meikle's shadow.

Our sons had left early in the day to climb toward three sheep they spied earlier from our front yard, but didn't know then that the sheep had also spotted them. The higher the boys climbed, the further up the mountain the sheep traveled. By dusk, Mark and Scott seemed no closer to them. They set up camp and slept until morning. At sunrise they jumped up to scan the ridges and located the sheep standing on a mountain on the opposite side of the valley.

After their breakfast, Mark and Scott crossed the valley. By lunchtime they reached the mountain where they had seen the sheep. They searched for them all that day, but never saw them again. Determined to find them the next morning, they camped again that night. When they finally spotted them, the sheep were back on the mountain where they had originally been seen, watching Mark and Scott. The boys decided to return home and try again another day.

On their way down the slopes, they saw two rams poised on a ridge far below them. Only one was legal. Scott took aim and fired. The ram remained standing. Convinced he missed, he shot again. The ram crumpled. Scrambling to the downed animal, they found both shots had entered the same hole. After dressing out the sheep, placing it in their backpacks, Mark and Scott made their weary way home just as the sun started its slide behind the ridges. Before entering the house they turned to look back up the mountain. There on a ridge watching them stood the three rams. The boys saluted them.

Remembering the day Scott brought a vole with a broken leg home to be fixed, I worried about his reaction to killing a sheep. Joe had told me men sometimes have problems with their first kill. Not wanting to make an issue of it I asked Scott, "You all right?" He nodded without saying anything. Still a hunter, he now takes his sons with him.

Our children knew and understood many secrets of the mountains, and Joe spent endless hours teaching them good marksmanship, how to respect, handle and care for guns, and where to place a deadly shot that destroyed little meat. "How about with a rock, Dad?" Scott asked, a big grin on his face. He had felled a grouse with one while he and Mark were hunting. They ate it that evening after roasting it over a campfire. "All right, Dead Eye, we're talking about hunting with guns," their father told him.

Joe had shown them how to slip a knife blade between hide and flesh to skin an animal. How to separate joints, and where the best cuts of meat could be found. He also taught them never to waste.

They knew how to build a shelter from storms, which wood provided the hottest fire, and to never hang meat close to camp. We were satisfied our boys could survive in the wilderness.

For myself, justifying taking a life has always been a problem, even believing as I do that certain animals are put here to provide food and clothing. However, if I had to kill to eat, I'd be a vegetarian – a naked vegetarian.

IDITAROD 2003

In 2003, the Iditarod race was a new experience for the personnel who create the logistics, the contestants, and me. To start with, because Alaska's weather did not cooperate and it was warm, and what little snow that fell had melted, the usual trail was changed to one not run previously by the mushers and their teams. The new course included 700 miles of running on frozen rivers: the Chena, the Tanana, and the Yukon.

In prior years when snow was plentiful, after mushing to Eagle River from downtown Anchorage where the Ceremonial Start takes place, participants loaded their dogs and drove to Wasilla for the Restart. That year, Wasilla had no snow. The Restart was moved to the Chena River in Fairbanks, and delayed a day to give mushers time to drive their teams 350 miles.

I've lost count of the Starts and Restarts I have attended, but never the feeling of excitement as I watched the teams leave at two-minute intervals. Up until 2003 it was a simple matter of driving to Anchorage or the designated area in Wasilla. Now, it meant a long trip up north.

Not wanting to spend hours in a car on slick, icy roads, my friend and I rode the Alaska Railroad Whistle- stop train from Wasilla to Fairbanks. That train comes to a standstill long enough for people living in remote areas along the tracks to unload groceries and building supplies. They can also ride to town to make purchases then catch the next train home. During our ten-hour ride we noticed a lack of snow, ice on the rivers, and open water.

At mile 174, the train stopped on the 550-foot bridge that spans Hurricane Gulch, with the Chulitna River approximately 280-feet below. It was a breathtaking experience for my friend who has a fear of heights.

Upon reaching Nenana, we were both relieved to see the river completely frozen over, and people erecting the Tripod for the Tanana Ice Classic, which is a yearly event. People bet on the exact time the ice goes out and the tripod topples.

By the time we reached Fairbanks, darkness had fallen.

A shuttle picked us up then drove to The Rivers Edge Resort. After a good night's sleep, we awoke to see snow on the ground, and the Chena River a few feet from our doorstep. It wasn't until we walked along the bank to Pike's Landing that we noticed open water in several places. That surprised us, as we knew mushers would be on the ice the following morning.

Kay, my friend, one of hundreds of volunteers helping with the race, a large percentage of whom live in other states, is from Michigan. While she attended a meeting to find out her duties in Fairbanks, I checked things out. I talked to people connected with the race and found nobody seemed too concerned about open water. "After all," as one person said to me, "The ice is fifteen inches thick, and mushers will keep their dogs clear of danger."

The day of the Restart at Pike's Landing, March 3, 2003, Kay's presence was required at 7 A.M. as a Crowd Controller. I arrived an hour before the Restart, amazed to see sixty-four trucks, each containing a dog team, media personnel, handlers, and spectators all out on the ice. Braving the river to take photos of mushers in jackets of red, blue, green, yellow, and black, and dogs in bright colored booties, I was careful to stay clear of open areas of water. The ice-free holes were clearly marked and some cordoned off to prevent accidents. As it was, we saw two people fall into the icy waters. Moving around I heard comments of, "What if the trucks fall through? How will they save the dogs? Do you think we should get off the river? How long would a person last if they fell in? Alaskans are crazy. They think they're indestructible."

Twenty minutes before the Restart, police, volunteers, and security people cleared spectators from the river. Competitors laid out dog harnesses, loaded sleds with food for themselves and their teams. Handlers placed booties on dogs that stood in pairs after being attached to the lines and sled. Mushers checked to see that no harnesses were tangled, and talked to their dogs. Their caring showed in the pats and soft voices they used, and the response they received. Some dogs, all four feet off the ground, jumped in place, howled, barked, and strained in their eagerness to be off. Enthusiasm rippled through the crowd.

Loaded down with my Pentax and Kay's video camera, I located a place to stand with an unobstructed view of the teams as they entered the chute, then made their way to the start line. Spectator anticipation increased. Loud speakers counted down the seconds to the time the teams would leave. Cheers for favorite contenders rang out. The dog-noise elevated.

Two and a half hours and a camera battery change later, the teams were on a course new to all, headed for Nome. Yells of encouragement faded as the teams rounded a bend in the river and moved out of sight. Spectators headed for a place to warm up and enjoy a hot drink. Trucks left the river. Police directed cars out of the parking lots. TV and radio personnel loaded up their gear and drove to Nenana to cover the arrival of the mushers at that first checkpoint. The Restart was over. With little advance notice, Fairbanks had excelled in its management of the race.

On our way back to our cottage, Kay and I ran into Susan Butcher, four-time winner of the Iditarod. Even though she and the owner of Pikes Landing were in a hurry, they kindly offered us a photographic opportunity. Three hours later we boarded our flight to Anchorage, then drove to Wasilla where Kay and I parted ways.

When the opportunity to go to Nome to see the mushers come in at the end of the race presented itself, I leapt at the chance. It was not until I stood close to the burled arch on Main Street and looked up at a blue lantern hanging there that I even knew one existed. The Blue Lantern, also known as The Widow's Lantern, was originally used during the days of sled dog freight and mail carrying. Because mushers ventured out in all manner of weather, they founded the idea for safety reasons. Word was sent out ahead that teams were on the trail. A kerosene lamp was lighted, hung outside the roadhouse and not extinguished until the musher safely reached his destination.

The Iditarod Trail Committee lighted the Blue Lantern on March 1, 2003, in Nome, where it remained until the last musher crossed the finish line. The lamp was then extinguished to signify the end of the race.

Some mushers quit along the way, and not all the dogs completed the race. Those animals that were lame, sick or injured remained at checkpoints, then were airlifted to Anchorage for veterinary care.

What a thrill to see men, women, and their amazing dogs after they traveled over a thousand miles. As I stood bundled up in all the winter clothing I possess, trying to fight cold winds whipping off the Bering Sea, my admiration for the participants increased. Not to diminish mushers in any way, I have to say, for me, the dogs are the real athletes.

Years ago, large, powerfully built mongrel dogs were used to haul gold from Nome, and carry U.S mail. They were the lifelines that connected isolated villages to the rest of the world and, of course, they carried medicine on the 674-mile diphtheria relay run from Nenana to Nome.

Nome is an unusual city. It is virtually crime free; after all, where can a criminal run? Many residents leave doors unlocked, don't worry about their children, and know their neighbors are there when needed. A nice friendly community. There are historical buildings rich with history from the gold rush era, and the era when dog teams brought 300,000 units of medicine to the diphtheria-plagued village in 1925.

One afternoon while waiting for mushers to come in, Kay and I attended an informative talk at the museum given by Howard Farley, who ran the first Iditarod race with Joe Redington in 1973. We also spent an interesting evening listening to Nadjda Soudakoua, a Russian Native, talk about the Inuit people of Far East Russia.

The Iditarod Trail has a history of its own. Segments of Native trails later became part the Iditarod Trail. American explorers and prospectors used those same routes. Impassable in summer, the frozen winter trail became the favorite passage. In 1908, the Alaska Road Commission surveyed, cleared and marked it. Dog mushing mailmen, freight services carrying supplies, and teams hauling gold shipments used it. For twenty years Iditarod was the main link between western communities in Alaska.

Dog teams, after delivering their cargo to Iditarod, were then laden with gold for their return trip. Between 1908 and 1925, approximately $35,000,000 in gold was extracted from the area. At that time it was worth $20 an ounce.

The town of Iditarod, from which the trail gets its name, was the center of the Iditarod Mining District, with a population of over 10,000. Today it is a ghost town.

THE WHISPER OF SNOWFLAKES

Our Alaskan winters have their own particular brand of pristine beauty: Northern Lights, frost covered trees, daggered kaleidoscopic icicles, crystal clear air, and the whisper of flakes lightly settling on snow-covered ground.

Have you ever heard a snowflake touch the earth? I have! It sounds like a butterfly landing on a blossom.

My husband Joe, our three children, and I lived miles from the nearest town. One Sunday afternoon, having been housebound for several days, we decided it was time to enjoy the snow that had built up over the last few weeks. And for the children to burn off some of their pent up energy. We climbed into our 4 X 4 truck and drove along the driveway, past the snow-people-family our children had created in the front yard; one member for each new snowfall.

The snow-people-family consisted of a group of misshapen individuals wearing jackets no longer fit for our family's use, but too small to button over a snowperson's fat belly. Each member looked out at his or her world through hockey puck eyes. Their clothes, some trimmed with scraps of fur, and gloves stuffed with straw. One displayed a flamboyant red and black-banded scarf hung around its neck, fashionably flung over a shoulder. Another dressed in our daughter's castoffs, a blue striped blouse over a green dress. The largest wore a plaid shirt and an old hat belonging to Joe. A frozen carrot nose, and large piano-key teeth finished the look desired by the children. Before winter's end, new members would join the ranks of sentries until warm days arrived.

At the end of our driveway, we turned on to an old rutted, mostly unused logging road, which ended at a stand of spruce set in among birch and aspen. Piling out of the vehicle we walked into an area close to a slough that few people visited during winter. There we could enjoy peace and tranquility.

Within an hour's stroll away from our truck, it started

snowing; a few flurries at first, then millions of big, fluffy flakes cascaded to earth. Bundled up in insulated suits, hats, gloves and snug fitting fur lined boots; neither the cold nor snow bothered us. Sounds were muted, the air becalmed. Evergreens dressed in winter finery, their boughs drooped with the weight of winter, deciduous trees stood stark naked except for an occasional leaf frozen in place, surrounded us. Animal tracks were being buried, but we could still see where a fox running between the trees had left a line of dainty prints, and the telltale trail – individual holes punched in the snow by high-stepping hooves – of a moose.

Further on, as it stood motionless at the base of a tree, we saw the shiny, ebony eyes and black trimmed ears of a snowshoe hare. Not far from us a red squirrel scampered down a spruce trunk then dashed off to it's midden, where it sat on its furry little bottom, folded its "hands," and admonished us for our intrusion. Above, we heard the swish of raven wings.

Ahead, our children played tag, running, rolling and pushing each other down. Reams of laughter and squeals of delight filled the air as they opened their mouths to catch a snowflake and feel it melt on their tongue. Leaving them to their games, Joe and I wandered off until we could no longer hear them. Finding an old, dead tree stump we sat to rest and wait for them to catch up.

It was so quiet there, so still. We heard snowflakes touching the ground as they landed. Maybe it was because we were straining to hear the children, or maybe it was one of those rare occasions when we blended with nature and our senses were acute. Is that not what the Creator intended?

Time passed quickly. It wasn't long before the quiet was totally shattered. Three boisterous, giggling, shouting youngsters, tumbled and stumbled into view. Ready to return home to the comfort of a crackling fire, dry clothes, hot chocolate and their most favorite "goody," Cranberry Dessert, they beckoned to us, yelling, "We're starving."

Before leaving the slough we stopped to watch a mink undulating like a Slinky toy on its way to open water, and an otter wriggling on its back like a Limbo dancer under a fallen branch. The children raced ahead as Joe and I strolled hand in hand back to our vehicle, each wrapped in our own thoughts. A moose and her yearling calf ventured out from between the trees, came into full view then vanished like a mirage.

Late that evening, sitting in front of the fire after the children had left for bed to dream their dreams, Joe and I discussed our day: the serenity and closeness of the moose mother and her calf, the playfulness of otters, and the fact that snowshoe hares change color to blend with their surroundings during every season. Our own feelings of contentment, and the magic of hearing a snowflake settle upon the earth.

Sometimes it is those small, enchanting moments we spend with the ones we love that are treasured lifetime memories.

The recipe in this story for our children's favorite goody evolved from pure desperation to find a different way to serve the cranberries we had spent hours gathering along hillsides in late summer. The whole milk was compliments of three goats belonging Scott, one younger son.

CRANBERRY DESSERT
2 Cups flour
1 Cup sugar
2 teaspoons baking powder
1 Cup cold whole milk
1 Tablespoon melted butter
2 1/2cups raw whole cranberries
1/2 Cup chopped walnuts (optional)

Preheat oven to 350 degrees. Combine in large mixing bowl, flour, sugar and baking powder. Stir in milk, melted butter, cranberries and walnuts. Mix well, then transfer into 2 ungreased 9-inch pie pans. Bake for 30 minutes. Do not remove from pans.

SAUCE
1 Cup sugar
1 stick butter (1/2 cup)
1 Cup evaporated milk
1 Teaspoon vanilla

To make sauce - Combine sugar, butter and evaporated milk in saucepan. Bring to boil and simmer for approximately 3 minutes. (Until sugar dissolves.) Remove from heat. Stir in vanilla. Pour sauce over cooked dessert in the 2 pans. Cut into wedges and serve while hot.

FAERIES AND THEIR ILK

My father, an Irishman, filled my young head with tales passed down from one generation to another of Mother Nature's helpers and mischief-makers. He called them "Wee People." I believed his every word as I looked into the depths of the foxglove held in his hand, where I saw all the proof I needed of Little People's existence--tiny faerie fingerprints dotting the inside of the silky, pinkish blossom.

Dad told me, "Foxes remove the blossoms then slip them onto their feet like gloves so they leave no tracks as they run to and from our chicken pen. When finished with their nighttime marauding, faeries help them replace the "gloves" back on the stalks as dawn lightens the morning sky."

In those years, my small child stature allowed me to crawl into lush colorful places where I could watch my little friends. Some dressed like hairy caterpillars with smiley faces, top hats and perky attitudes. Others wore yellow and black striped suits and hummed while they worked collecting honey from fragrant blossoms and flowering shrubs. And there were those who fluttered in the scented air on bright orange or spotted wings. They all played hide and seek. I loved those Wee People who dwelt in my enchanted world.

My mother, a gentle smile on her face, permitted me to eat my lunch outside and to share it with my garden friends. I left them crumbs or a dab of icing where they could find it. When I checked later it was always gone. Secretive in their ways, I never saw them carry away the gifts I left on a moss covered tree stump; nor did I ever catch them nibbling.

The night I discovered an in-house elf, he was as surprised as I. Intently occupied with some mischief, he apparently did not hear me enter my bedroom. I giggled at the sight of him in his little red hat and matching pants, green shirt and yellow pointed shoes. With a puckish caught-in-the-act smile that also seemed conspiratorial on his face, he suddenly jumped up, danced to the sound of silver bells on his feet, stopped, shrugged his tiny shoulders and winked at me. Then, in an instant, he floated to the open window in a misty cloud; and vanished.

At breakfast the following morning, I chattered to my parents about my experience, thinking they'd be as excited as I. My mother patted me on the head and said, "That's nice."

My father, who I was convinced knew everything, gave me a knowing look, then said, "You, me darlin' daughter, had the good fortune to meet a genuine, "They."

"You know who "They" are?" he queried.

Before I could think of a response, he answered his own question.

"They," my child, are who hide things like my car keys so I can't find them. "They" make the cat's hair stand on end when we can see no reason for it. "They" return empty milk jugs to the fridge and, "They" encourage you to get into mischief by doing what we told you not to. "They" are the ones YOU blame when you tell your mother and me, "I don't know. "They" must have done it."

Years later as a teenager, I wandered down to the copse near the wild end of my parent's English garden just before dusk on warm summer evenings. There, I listened to Music Faeries playing with bluebells that tinkled in the clear evening air. I noticed where Leprechauns had closed the Irish Shamrock blossoms for the night, and a faerie ring of brown toadstools where they held a party. Deeper in the woods, Artist People had decorated handsome, bright red-orange mushrooms with white dots that stood in small, clusters on the woodland floor.

Now an adult, I still leave a jigger of Irish Mist under the Gnome home on my lawn for the Leprechauns. It's their favorite beverage. On moonlit nights they-gnomes, pixies, elves and others of their ilk gather to celebrate life. Sometimes if I'm exceptionally lucky, I catch a quick glimpse of them dressed in green suits and purple tri-pointed hats before they disappear. They are shy when they dance, but the next morning I find evidence of their celebration. Hidden among my flowerbeds are miniscule footprints of different shapes and sizes: some pointed, others three-toed, and still others; diminutive replicas of my own bare feet.

Another group of Wee People I have encountered over

time are the Dream Sprites. Happy, playful little wraithlike persons dressed in white. They sit on my bookcase headboard. They filter my thoughts and wishes; then, when I fall asleep, they whisk me away to places my body cannot go.

One night they spirited me away to the Serengeti, where I walked amid herds of elephant, wildebeest, gazelle and zebra. Trying to tempt a puppy-size zebra baby to come to me, I held out my hand. He trotted forward. My heart fluttered with excitement. Suddenly, this picture perfect miniature spun around, jumped in the air and kicked out with his hind feet. Tiny black hooves flashed in the moonlight. I jerked back – and fell out of bed. Dream Sprite's tinkling laughter filled the silence of my room.

Around my home in Alaska, Frost Faeries sprinkle snow with glittering diamonds, and point the way for the wind to clear snow from frozen lakes and rivers so the moon will reflect on polished ice. They create rainbow-gathering icicles, which sound like wind chimes when they shatter on the ground, and hurl bright stars across the heavens. They gather ice crystals in the shape of colorful sundogs to guard the winter sun.

These same faeries dress the evergreens in winter white finery and breathe hoarfrosts onto the tiniest of twigs. With grace and spontaneity they spin in rapid circles while dancing whirling jigs on mountaintops, spiraling snow ever higher into the sky. On dark nights, above the luminescent snowcapped peaks, they sensuously waltz across the heavens in long, flowing green, red, blue and wispy cream-colored robes. They also help to protect hibernating seeds and animals beneath the frozen ground until sun-warmed days arrive.

Spring and summer bring the Flower faeries. Their slim, lithe forms arrive on backs of dragonflies edging toward streams that murmur their way to Lily pad-filled ponds, or on the vibrant velvet wings of butterflies, or they daintily sit astride the furry shoulders of a bee. They beautify my garden, the woodlands, lakes, and tundra with radiant multihued flora. Evidence of their influence is everywhere.

Then there are the two-toed, bulbous nosed, bulging eyed, liver-lipped, treacherous Trolls who belong to the hobgoblin mischief-maker family. They live in the inner workings of my computer. Playing hopscotch on my keyboard they fling 'Access Denied' and other messages I don't know what to do about when they suddenly pop up on my screen. I watch the keys as I type but never catch them at their dastardly deeds. Without success, I vacuum the ventilation holes in my machine's casing trying to suck them out. I have no idea how they found their way into my office all these miles from under a bridge in Scandinavia, but I'd be delighted if they'd return to their motherland.

As you can tell, even now as a senior Alaskan Sourdough, I still believe in faerie tales, and unlike the Apostle Paul, I did not put away childish things when I became an adult. That's why I talk to my plants; hear whispers in the trees when a breeze brushes its way through leafy branches. See pearly bubbles pushed from its depths by Water Nymphs after poking my finger into the glassy surface of a lake. And, at those times I fear something I don't comprehend, and the hair on my arms stands at attention. I never question the existence of imps.

GOLDIE HORSE

Goldie was an elderly lady when we inherited her with property we purchased. Sixteen hands high, swaybacked, and independent, she was as comfortable as a rocking chair to sit astride. She reminded us of the cartoon horse, Epic, in the Tumbleweed cartoon. We had to chase her to catch her if we wanted a ride.

She was abandoned by her previous owners and had spent a winter fending for herself, eating willows and whatever else she found. With no shelter and no company, she withstood temperatures of 60 below zero and colder. Originally there had been three horses. The other two died; one from starvation, the other, bear-killed.

The boys made a pack for Goldie. While they worked, she watched until it was finished, then ran off. They chased her, caught her, strapped the pack on her back, then ran to the house to tell us they were leaving on a trip up the valley to haul petrified wood. By the time they made their way back to Goldie, she'd wriggled out of the pack. Off they raced to tether her again. They cinched the girth tighter around her middle. As they walked away from the house, Goldie expelled the air she'd sucked in before they tightened the girth; off fell the pack. Finally they outsmarted her.

Thinking the hike too long for their sister to make in both directions, the boys hefted her onto Goldie's back. Our dogs followed the little group that looked like original sourdoughs heading for the hills. Late that night they returned. The only one not carrying a load of petrified wood was Goldie. They told us, she had acted like a jackass instead of a packhorse. Squeezing herself between trees, she had wiped off her pack.

And when one of our children rode her, she deliberately walked under low hanging branches to dislodge them. They said they felt like making her into hamburger, but decided they loved her too much, even if she hadn't been any help to them. She remained home after that trip. They still managed to bring down enough petrified wood to sell at twenty-five cents a pound to buy two snowmobiles.

Over the years Goldie became more and more of a barn-sow. When we rode her, she slowly plodded along on the outward journey like she could hardly make it. On the way home she raced like a Triple Crown contender.

She lived with us until she was about seventeen years old and then trotted off to the big meadow in the sky.

A BUSH CHRISTMAS

Loaded with gifts wrapped in bright colored paper, my parents arrived in Anchorage from England, to spend six weeks with us and celebrate the holiday season. It was their first visit to Alaska in winter, and twenty years since I had shared a Christmas with them. Mom and Dad had previously spent one summer at our farm outside Fairbanks, which they enjoyed except for my father's stay in the hospital from blood poisoning caused by too many mosquito bites.

The years we had been apart I wrote to my parents on a weekly basis trying to describe the breath-taking scenery, the warm short spring, and the long, sunshiny days of summers. Needing to convince them our decision to move to the Far North was right, I had played down the severity of winter. I also knew that reading about the cold and snow, and experiencing it were two different things. Southern England seldom sees snow.

We picked them at the airport. Settled in the for the journey home Joe said, "As you know we've moved from Fairbanks. I hope you'll like where we chose."

My parents had not seen our log house or the lifestyle we lived. It was very different from their own home, with all modern conveniences, in the small village where they moved to after selling their farm. My parents asked a thousand questions, commented on the beauty of the snow-covered mountains, the ice crystals floating in the air, the slick roads and, of course, how the children had grown.

After a great deal of catching up, my father said, "A nice hot bath will feel good after all the hours of sitting." I hastily changed the subject in hopes of keeping my husband or children from prolonging that conversation. Luckily, by the time Mom and Dad settled in, they decided to forego a bath and retire for the night.

The following day turned out to be typical for the Interior, with a spectacular sunrise of rose pink, reddish orange, and deep red. The sun floated in a forget-me-not blue sky, and tipped the snow-laden evergreen boughs in gold. In early afternoon it slipped behind the mountains. Watching the sunset, my mother commented, "It's beautiful. Looks just like some of the Christmas cards you sent."

The weather stayed clear for most of Mom and Dad's six-weeks visit. Only occasionally did clouds gather and unload their cargo to ground already covered with three feet of snow. That particular winter was one of the mildest I had spent in Alaska; however, the thirty-five-below-zero temperature shocked my parents.

Miles from modern conveniences, we not only lacked running water, we also lived without electricity. We melted snow on a barrel stove or hauled water in fifty-five gallon drums from the river. My parents thought both methods uncouth, and the way we lived, uncivilized. I had hoped that was not going to be the case. Had they forgotten I grew up on their farm without electricity and running water? After a few grumbles, they accepted the inconvenience and having to use the Port-a-potty we acquired for them. I thought the trek to the outhouse was more than they should have to endure.

Neither of my parents took kindly to the wild critters in our house. We had a duck with frozen feet, a caged mink in the kitchen, and a southern-migrating hawk that hadn't healed in time for release before cold weather set in. A three-legged fox that roamed free. An eagle perched on a tree limb we brought in, its broken wing set and taped to its body. Then, to add to the menagerie, Scott's nanny goat and one of my ewes gave birth to twins on Christmas Eve. We moved the four babies into the house to bottle-feed and keep warm. Their mothers had refused to nurse them.

One morning the duck waddled under the table to pick up scraps. My father nudged it out of the way with his foot. The eagle hopped onto the mink cage, causing uproar. It seemed I spent hours trying to justify why these critters needed to be in the house. I hoped parents understood my need to help the sick, injured, and helpless animals.

That evening, sitting all together after listening to their thoughts on the subject once again, I asked, "Don't you remember Salina, my pet pig? She slept on a rug beside my bed. You didn't mind that." Instantly, our children's eyes lit up. They wanted to hear the story. "As a runt piglet, her mother stepped on her and broke her leg," I told them. "Grandma said I could keep her as long as I promised to take care of her." I noticed my parents smiling at one another, and sensed they were recapturing days long past at their farm before it sold and they moved into their home with a small garden spot.

My mother told the children about a Christmas when she and my Dad were first married. "I remember he brought me home a white rat. My mother apparently felt the same way about that rat as I do about your animals."

Janny asked, "Did you keep it, Grandma?"

"Oh my, yes. I had him until he died of old age. His name was Whiskers."

"Did your mother ever learn to like him?"

"No, but she stopped complaining about him when I told her how much I loved him."

"You'll love Mom's critters, too, Grandma." Jan said, as she picked up the duck.

After a new snowfall a few days later, my eighty-two year old father stood at the kitchen window watching our sons riding their snowmobiles. He turned to my husband, and said, "I'd like to try that."

"Act your age, Sam. You're not as young as you think you are. You'll break your neck," my mother scolded. Her words did nothing to dissuade him.

An hour later, our sons, Mark and Scott, returned, raced into the house, closed the door behind them, and shed their snowsuits. They scrambled to the table and proceeded to devour a stack of pancakes, eggs, and moose steak. After they'd eaten and cleared away their dishes, they helped their father and I bundle up my Dad in layer upon layer of warm clothes, then Joe walked out with him to explain the mechanics of the machine.

At first Dad drove slowly and cautiously, but two days later he was speeding along the trails behind his grandchildren. Upon their return, my Dad, while standing with his back to the woodstove, glanced at my mother. "Exhilarating," he said. My mother looked at him, shaking her head.

After thawing out, Dad removed the parka; facemask, mittens, and white insulated boots, then wrapped his hands around a cup of hot soup. His bright eyes showed his happiness.

As Christmas neared, the house filled with whispered secrets. We were all crafting homemade gifts. Five days before the holiday arrived, Joe and our daughter, as was their ritual every year, left to gather our tree. Before they walked out the door, Grandma gave them strict instructions as to what size and shape they should bring home. Joe smiled knowing he'd never find what she described, not among the black spruce in our area.

When they returned dragging a tree-loaded sled behind the snowmachine, I listened to Joe laughing and Janny giggling as they parked by the backdoor. Janny, buried under the tree and caked with snow kicked up by the machine's track, rolled off the sled. She stood, shook off as much snow as possible then, like a robot, walked stiff-legged into the house.

Later in the day, the family gathered in the living room to stand the tree in its holder. The scent of the freshly cut spruce filled the house. That evening we decorated it. Homemade and store bought ornaments hung amid shimmering tinsel from its branches. Beneath the boughs were stacked packages wrapped in paper decorated by our children. The lingering aroma of pies my mother baked earlier in the wood cook stove drifted from the kitchen. Dancing flames from the fire reflected on the log walls. Softly sung carols from our battery-operated radio played in the background.

Curled up with his eyes covered by his tail, Tigger, Janny's tiger-striped cat, slept in the old rocking chair Joe made for me as an anniversary gift in the third year of our marriage. Kodiak, my dog, sprawled out on the floor in front of the fire. Puff, Janny's poodle, investigated the packages under the tree, and Grandma and Grandpa sat side by side on the couch. For me it completed the picture of what Christmas should be; a house filled with the family I love.

Our children's miniature Christmas tree, planted in a moss green pottery planter set on a linen doily, decorated the center of our dining room table. Golden-crusted pies, and still warm cinnamon rolls cooled on the kitchen counter. Oven ready, a homegrown turkey stuffed with my family's favorite dressing of sausage, applesauce, breadcrumbs and herbs, sat next to them.

Late that night, Joe sat crossed legged on the floor, assembling new rifles bought for our sons. My projects completed, I handed him parts and pieces he needed. Our children snuggled under their quilts slept peacefully, oblivious of what was waiting for them beneath the tree the next morning.

After my parents retired for the night, Joe and I sat reminiscing about Christmas' in our childhood. I laughed as I recalled a long ago Christmas Eve when I crept from my bedroom and hid under the piano in the living room. From my hiding place, I spied on my parents wrapping packages and placing them under the tree. Finally, after I thought they had gone to bed and fallen asleep, I quietly opened the door, intending to return to my room without my parent's knowledge. I collided with my mother. We both jumped. I received a lecture and a swat on my bottom for sneaking around.

Early the next morning my father handed me my first gift - a colorfully wrapped box - containing a lump of coal!

Joe laughed. "Just what you deserved."

"Well, I didn't think so. I was a child." I said. "I cried."

Joe, raised in Iowa, sipped his hot cider before saying, "The Christmas I remember most was when I was twelve and Dad gave me my first gun, a Stevens 22 rifle," he said. "He, my brother, and I went hunting while Mom cooked dinner. I shot my first pheasant that day. The family made such a big deal over it I felt ten feet tall."

Our stories continued late into the night. As we rose from in front of the fire to head for bed, Bunny, a Snowshoe hare we raised from a tiny baby, hopped onto a log we used as a stool. He stood on his hind feet and sniffed the needles on the tree. "I'll never forget this Christmas," I told Joe as we watched him.

"I wonder which one our kids will carry in their hearts," Joe said with a smile. "Well, best get to bed. They'll be up in a couple of hours"

Frantic to share the happiest of days, Mark, Scott, and Jan impatiently waited for all year, they raced into our bedroom and jumped on the bed. "Come on Mom, Dad. It's time to get up," they said between giggles and laughter.

"I hope you didn't wake your grandparents," I said just as my father called a cheerful, "Morning."

Joe looked at the clock. It was 5.30 a.m.

Over breakfast, Jan asked, "Mom, is it true animals can talk at midnight on Christmas Eve?"

"I've never heard them, Sweetheart," I said. 'It would be nice, though, if they told us how they feel and what they think."

The weeks between Christmas and the time my parents returned to England, we played games or sat talking in the evenings. I heard our children asking them the same questions I asked at their age, and listened to the same answers I had received. Do all children have the same thoughts, I wondered?

On New Year's Eve, my parents, who had never seen Northern Lights, stood outside wrapped in coats and heavy blankets. They looked up in awe as red, green and ivory white gossamer strands swayed, swirled and danced across the sky. My father turned to speak to my mother. At that instant a wolf howled, its voice echoing down the valley. Dad's thoughts seemed to filter away in the crisp air.

In the silence that followed, he reached for my hand and whispered, "Now I understand why you chose this place."

I turned, hugged him and said, "I so hoped you would, Dad."

MY HALIBUT FISHING TRIP

At sixty some years old I still had not outgrown my inability to sleep the night before a trip. I can still remember my parents coming into my bedroom several times the night before a planned trip and telling me, "Go to sleep. You'll be grumpy in the morning if you don't." Of course, I assured them, "I'll be my perky little self. Promise." That's what I said, but ended up being cranky, anyway.

The same kind of excitement and anticipation kept me awake most of the night before the halibut-fishing trip that was coming up the following morning. After all, it was going to be a new experience for me.

My son Scott, and his father-in-law, Jack, picked me up on the way to Wasilla airport, where we climbed into the small plane waiting on the runway. Mark, my oldest son, piloted the aircraft. I love flying in small planes, especially when he is the pilot. From on high, sights that remain a mystery to those who are earthbound are revealed. The moment the plane lifts from the ground to streak through the boundless sky, a surge of adrenaline rushes through me and my heart skips a pulse at the magic of seeing the world from a bird's eye view.

Always, as we cruise through the air, the poem, High Flight, written by a young American in the Canadian Air Force, killed in England in 1941, runs through my head.

High Flight
Oh! I have slipped the surly bonds of earth
And danced the skies on laughter-silvered wings
Sunward I've climbed, and joined the tumbling mirth
Of sunlit clouds - - and done a thousand things
You have not dreamed of - - wheeled and soared
And swung high in sunlit silence.
Hov'ring there I've chased the shouting wind alone,
And flung my eager craft through footless halls of air.

Up, up the long delirious, burning blue,
I've topped the windless heights with easy grace
Where never lark, or even eagle flew - -
And, while with silent lifting mind I've trod
The high-untrespassed sanctity of space,
Put out my hand and touched the face of God.

I wondered, does Mark have those same thoughts and feelings as he sits at the controls?

Daylight had barely broken the morning sky as we rose from the ground headed for Homer. We soared above glaciers that could be seen no other way, rugged mountains and mile after mile of uninhabited land. Looked down on a flock of flying swans. Saw goats, moose, bears, and sheep on hillsides. We watched Beluga whales in the glacial silt filled waters of Cook Inlet far below us. Then, all too soon, Kachemak Bay appeared beneath the right wing. We were almost at our destination.

Along with other patrons eagerly waiting to head out to sea we boarded a charter fishing boat in Homer. At the push of a button the engines kicked in, then roared as we eased away from the dock. Small talk stopped. On our way to where several fishing boats were already anchored, anticipation ran rampant as we rode the waves along a golden swath painted by the rising sun. As we drew close to other boats the engines quieted. We heard excited voices of men and women waiting to wet their line and try their luck. Suddenly, a loud yell of, "I've got one on," rose above the chatter. All heads swiveled toward the woman. The captain of that boat ran over to help reel her catch up through the choppy water. An excited, "Yes!" filled the air from a man who struggled to hoist a huge gaffed halibut over the rails and onto the deck of yet another boat.

Finally, our boat edged closer and jostled its way into place. A crewmember threw the anchor overboard. The male clients on board baited up and threw their lines over the side. The captain gouged the hook at the end of my line into a baitfish. I was not only the lone female in the group, but also had the only head of white hair.

"It'll be a long haul, Ma'am. We're fishing at two hundred fifty feet," he said as he handed me the pole.

Having no idea what that meant I replied with a jaunty smile, "No problem."

While my line, with its three-pound weight, sank out of sight, Scott had his first bite. With what looked like little effort he dragged up a halibut weighing forty-three pounds. (We found that out after we returned to the dock.) Mark had one on. Jack was pulling one in. People on other boats were screaming excited remarks as they hauled up fish of various sizes, while I contentedly waited for something to grab my bait. Then it happened. The pole moved in my hand. I felt a tug on my line. Three voices yelled at me in unison, "Set the hook."

"How?" I shouted back.

With that the captain dropped what he was doing, ran over, unceremoniously grabbed my pole, set the hook, then walked away saying, "Reel 'er in."

My sons watched as I worked the reel.

"Need help, Mom?" Mark asked.

"Nah. It's a breeze," I said. I wasn't about to tell him my arms already ached.

Jack hooked another one. Mark hauled one over the rail. Scott had one on. I was still reeling, but slower now.

"I'll give you a break," Scott offered.

"No, it's almost to the surface." That's what I thought. I was wrong. Two hundred fifty feet is a long way down.

By the time my fish was half way to the surface, I was positive the ocean floor was attached to my hook. After a few more minutes of cranking, both hands cramped and my arms, feeling like they were about to drop off, left me having to take an offer of help. I passed my pole to my son. As I watched intently, I first saw the flat, bug-eyed, gray mottle back rising from the depths. Then, as the fish started to battle the hook, I saw the white-bellied mass rising in the clear turquoise water.

Immediately, a rush of regret race through my mind; I wanted it to break free. I think I'd have become bait if I'd uttered my thoughts aloud. On deck, the poor fish flipped and flopped until a crewmember placed it in a box along with all those caught so far.

Some of the other boats left once customers had caught their limit, but returned in a few hours with new clients on board. Both my sons had their limit. Jack was hauling in the last one of his quota, while I, completely worn out, struggled with my last fish. As much as I hated to allow it, my sons brought it the remainder of the way up but, with help, I managed to haul it over the rail onto the deck. By the time it went to the box, I don't know who looked more dead, the fish or I.

On the trip back to the harbor we saw round, fuzzy headed otters. One of them disappeared underwater then surfaced with a big crab, which after flipping onto its back the otter ate. Another pair of otters frolicked in a floating bed of kelp. Black and white dolphins, look-ing like miniature Orcas sped along beside the boat, then in front, and then in the wake, finally rolling away with bounding leaps. Closer to land, Bald eagles soared then plummeted, legs extended, talons ready, toward salmon in the water, which, once caught, the bird then turned the head to point forward in a position of least resistance. Seagulls, their cries rising above all other sounds flocked around the boats unloading their catch.

After our boat tied up, I struggled onto the dock while the men, still full of energy, hopped out of the boat. All the fish caught by people in our party were weighed. Jack caught the biggest fish of the day, a 145 pounder. It looked as big as my front door. Next Mark, then Scott. Catching the smallest halibut in our family gave me no shame. My total catch weighed 122lbs. Considering how hard I worked to hoist them up from the bottom of the ocean, I was proud of myself even though I had to have help. Between the four of us and the fish, we weighed too much for the small plane to safely carry home. I offered to go commercial, but I was not heavy enough to offset the needed poundage.

I sat next to Mark on the flight back to Wasilla. Scott, behind us, kept the hundreds of pounds of filleted hali-but company. Jack flew on a commercial airline. Tired by the time we landed at Wasilla airport, none of us looked forward to cutting and wrapping our catch to set in our freezers. But, invigorated once we started telling tall fish tales, we forgot how tired we were.

Late that night, exhausted, muscles aching, I fell into bed and dreamed I caught a halibut the size of my kitchen table. Struggling and straining to bring it to the surface I awoke to the sound of my own voice saying, "No, I don't need help! It's just a fish."

SNOWMEN

In January, the first heavy snowfall arrived. To begin with only a few flakes drifted down but by nightfall it was snowing hard. Our house in the mountains, protective and peaceful, snuggled around us while it continued snowing for more three days.

For my family the three-foot snowfall meant shoveling the roof, clearing pathways, and building new snowmen. The snow-people-family already built consisted of a group of misshapen individuals wearing clothes no longer fit for our family to use, but too small to button over a snowperson's fat belly. Each member looked out at his or her world through hockey puck eyes. They wore hats trimmed with scraps of fur, and gloves stuffed with straw. A red and black-banded scarf hung around their neck, with one end fashionably flung over a shoulder. Above the scarf was a frozen carrot nose and a huge toothy smile. Before winter's end the family would be joined by new members: large, small, and in between.

After spending part of the day adding to the snow-people-family, my family decided they wanted a moose roast for dinner that night. I dug one out of the shed where, in winter, we kept our frozen meat protected from wildlife. Stuffing garlic cloves deep into the meat, sprinkling it with thyme, onion and garlic salt, I added a bay leaf or two, plus pieces of beef suet, which we had bought on our yearly shopping trip. After covering the pan the roast was in with foil, I slipped it into the oven of our wood stove. Hot temperature seared the outside of the meat and sealed in the juices. Then, as the fire burned down, the oven cooled and the meat cooked slowly. The house filled with luscious smells. Later I made bread, peeled potatoes, and opened a jar of vegetables canned earlier.

We never wasted what we hunted. We ate the meat, the bones and scraps went to Kodiak and the other dogs, plus we tanned the hide.

As I removed bread from the oven two hours later, our kids, who had returned to the outside, ran into the house after completing one more snow-child. Their timing was perfect. Maybe the aroma had drifted to them. As was their habit, they took a loaf each, split it in half lengthways, slathered it with butter and jelly then disappeared until called for dinner.

DEAR WORLD

The principal called with news. Good news. Our son Scott was to graduate valedictorian. So proud of him that I needed to do something beside tell him my feelings I sat down and wrote the following to be read at graduation. Originally I intended to write only for him, but as I thought about the content of the letter, the more I realized it meant all those boys and girls would be entering a world of unknowns. As parents we would no longer be there on a daily basis to guide them, advise them or care for them while they were away at college. And so, I wrote the following letter to be read at the graduation ceremony.

Dear World.
Our children finish school today. It's all going to be quite strange to them for a while, and I wish you would treat them kindly.

You see up to now they have been king of their roost and their parents have always been near to soothe their wounds and repair their feelings. Now things are going to be different. They are starting out on a new adventure.. It is an adventure that may include war, tragedy and sorrow. To make their way in the world they will have to live in will require a great deal of faith, love, tolerance and understanding.

So, World, I wish you would look after them. Take them by the hand and teach them the things they will need to know, but please World do it gently if you can. They will have to learn that not all people are just, that not all people are fair, and that not all people are true. But also teach him or her that for every villain there is a hero. That for every crooked politician there is a great and dedicated leader. Teach them also that for every enemy there is a good friend.

It will take time World, but teach them that a nickel earned is of more value than a dollar found. Teach them to lose gracefully, so that they will enjoy winning that much more.

Steer them away from envy if you can, and teach them the secret of quiet laughter. Teach them to be at peace with their God. Teach them to be strong inside so they can stand the hurt of failure and keep the desire to try again until they succeed. Teach them to be gentle with gentle people and to be tough with tough people.

Teach them to follow their judgments and not the crowd. Teach them to listen to all people, but to filter all they hear through a screen of truth and take the good that siphons through.

Teach them to laugh when they are sad, but also teach them that there is no shame in tears. Teach them there can be glory in failure and despair in success.

Teach them to disregard cynics and to beware of too much sweetness. Teach them to sell their brains and brawn to the highest bidder, but to never put a price on their heart and soul.

Teach them if you can, not to compare themselves with others. There will always be greater or lesser persons. Teach them instead to surpass their own accomplishments.

Teach them there is a time to gamble, but there is also a time to pass the dice.

Treat them gently World, but don't coddle them. Only the test of fire makes the finest steel. Teach them to have sublime faith in themselves, as this will give them faith in mankind.

This is quite an order World, but see what you can do. They are such nice young people - our children.

CABIN FEVER

Come about February or March, a lot of people who live in Alaska become victims of Cabin Fever, which manifests itself in several ways. Some residents become restless, while others sink into the doldrums.

I suffer from the restlessness symptom. I've lived in Alaska for many years now, and when March arrives I'm ready to get out and plant my garden. What I have in mind are lilacs, tulips and daffodils but, of course, the only things that would survive that early in the year are icicles!

In the dead of winter, people who work outside the home, and children attending school, see daylight only on their days off. My husband used to say, "I feel like coming home and hanging myself upside down in the closet like a bat!"

One cold, cloudy day while searching for something practical to do instead of aimlessly pacing from room to room picking up magazines I couldn't settle to read, I stumbled on an old recipe sent to me twenty years ago by a friend who had lived in the Alaska bush. She had despaired over the winter blahs she dealt with every year. As well as all the things she accomplished to make it through those times, she developed an offbeat sense of humor.

This is the recipe she sent me:

ALASKAN CABIN FEVER CAKE.

1 Cup Sugar
3 Fifths Rum
1 Cup Dried Fruit
2 Cups brown sugar
1 Tsp baking soda
1 Cup butter
2 Large eggs
1 tsp baking powder
Lemon juice
2 Cups Walnuts

Before starting, sample rum to check quality. Good isn't it?

Now proceed.

Select large mixing bowl, measuring cup, etc. Check rum again. It must be just right. To be sure rum is of proper quality, pour 1 level cup of rum into glass and drink as fast as you can.

Repeat above rum instructions.

Then, with electric mixer, beat 1 Cup butter in large and fluffy bowl. Add 1 teaspoon of Thugar and beat again. Meanwhile, make sure rum is still all right. Open another fifth and try another cup or two. Open third fifth if necessary. Drink one more cup.

Add eggs, 2 Cups fried druit, and heat until high. If druit gets stuck in the beaters, pry loose with drewsscriber.

Sample rum again, checking for tonscisticity. Next, sift 3 cups of pepper or salt, (really doesn't matter.) Sample rum again. Then sift 1/2 Pint of Lemon juice. Fold in Chopped Butter and Strained Nuts. Add 1 Babblespoon of Brown Thugar or whatever color you can find.

Wix Mell.

Grease oven. Turn cake pan 350 degrees. Pour mess into boven and ake.

Check rum again, then fall into bed!!

Along with this crazy recipe, my friend tried to warn me of the affliction that comes with short days, long nights and perpetual snow, but in my youthful ignorance I didn't think I'd ever have to worry about such trivia. After all, I intended to enjoy winter, snowmobiling, skating, painting and long moonlit walks under swirling northern lights, bundled up in a warm parka, mittens and boots that would stand forty below zero, naturally.

The first couple of winters flew by, the third seemed to take a little longer and the fourth dragged. By the time fall rolled around and winter stared us in the face the fifth year, I found myself dreading the coming months. Two years later I had a full-blown attack of Cabin Fever.

At first I thought I was coming down with the flu bug, but I didn't have headache, fever, aches or pains. I couldn't sleep, yet couldn't seem to work up any enthusiasm for much of anything. Even a full moon rising over snow covered peaks, bathing the world in clamshell light lost its magic. I was tempted to try my friend's recipe.

Instead, over the years, I learned to cook typical Alaskan fare, moose, salmon, halibut, caribou, and sheep. I'd also either invented or been given recipes for several liqueurs made from wild berries, which slid down well on long winter evenings sitting in front of a log fire.

After a few more years passed, I spent the dreary months drooling over pictures of sandy beaches and warm Caribbean waters, but we never seemed to have enough money to go to those places. To pass the time I found new crafts to fill my days: woodcarving, writing, ceramics, and placing years of pictures stored in a box into albums.

The good thing about Cabin Fever is it only lasts a reasonably short period of time. When May arrives, it's time to start planting seeds in pots in the house, and with the promise of spring, the winter dilemma starts to fade. Spirits pick up as each day gains five minutes of extra sunlight until June's Summer Solstice. At that time, the nights consist of dusk, and the sun holds real heat, no longer just the illusion of warmth.

During the first week of June, I rush to plant my carefully nurtured seedlings in flowerbeds, or transplant tomatoes into the greenhouses. After a day's work outside I relax on the deck, sit in a lawn chair next to a barbeque cooking salmon. The aroma wafts over to the neighbors yard. They invite themselves over and we sip our diminishing supply of beverages made the previous fall.

Our animated conversation, interrupted by swatting at mosquitoes, turns to the joys of nineteen-hour sunny days, boating, camping, fishing, and gardening. Winter is weeks behind us, and Cabin Fever long forgotten.

OUR WILDERNESS HOME

The evening we left our farm outside Fairbanks, Tippy, the three-legged fox we'd had in our care, sat on a berm watching us. He looked healthy but shaggy in his summer coat. Joe and the boys had left ahead of Janny, Sandy, a dog belonging to a friend, Puff, and Kodiak, and me.

I knew I should hurry with my final check through the house, but I dawdled. Memories flooded my mind: happy hours in front of the fire, operating on sick birds and animals on the kitchen table, the sound of our children's laughter, the times Joe and I held hands in front of the fire. The canoe we filled with water so Mama and Papa Goose could have a pool to paddle in. The day we found the old house in need of a family. And, even though the future we had searched for was out there waiting, sadness filled me.

Finally, I made myself climb into the car, glad of the dim interior to hide my tears. Janny, cuddled up on the back seat with her poodle Puff, and Sandy had fallen asleep. Kodiak, always non-judgmental, licked my face. Level with my favorite fox I stopped and rolled down the window to say goodbye.

Sometimes in my dreams I see him surrounded by his mate and snub nosed, short-legged, fat kits in a den by the slough. In my dreams, he lets me sit with him, handle his babies, share his family. Dreams...

The first days in our wilderness home we spent unpacking boxes, trying to find a place for our belongings. Mark and Scott took theirs to their own cabins. Janny decided to live in the house and have a cabin for play. There were more than enough cabins to go around. Joe needed one for his tools and a place to call his own, and I had to have a place to call mine. Eventually we arranged it that way, but to begin with things were disastrous. We all shoved stuff we couldn't find an immediate home for in cabin number four. To open that door was to invite an avalanche.

We had a paradise of lakes, ponds, mountains, and wildlife, no close neighbors, no electricity, and no running water. Cold or hot, we trekked to the outhouse when Mother Nature called. In winter our trips were hurried and we didn't sit around making wishes over a Sears and Roebuck catalogue, or reading a good book. Nor did we dally in the summer when mosquitoes threatened.

For me, the move to the bush was the culmination of a dream. As a teenager I'd read every book I could find on living a remote life, spent hours drooling over all it offered. The book, "Mrs. Mike," by B. and N. Freedman, I read and re-read at least a dozen times, thinking the life she lived was the ultimate.

The life we led was the ultimate for us. Our friends, on the other hand, found isolation unfamiliar and uncomfortable. We worked hard all summer preparing for the cold months of long winters. We planted and cared for an acre garden, fished, cut wood, grew tomatoes and cukes in our greenhouse, raised chickens for eggs, and turkeys for meat. Late summer provided us with an abundance of wild berries waiting to be picked for baking and jelly making.

We canned our vegetables when summer ended and fall slid into our valley. During hunting season, Janny and I bird-dogged for our men folk while they hunted for moose, sheep, hare, grouse, and ptarmigan.

Once winter arrived things settled down, but we remained busy. The domestic sheep, goats, dogs, cat, chickens, turkeys, the horse we inherited with the property, and a mule named Jasper, that we brought with us from Fairbanks, all needed tending. The children took home schooling, which meant lessons needed to be completed on schedule. We all created crafts; wood clocks with Alaskan animals burnt into the surface, burl end tables, and antler jewelry. I painted Alaskan scenery that Joe framed. These things we sold at different stores and lodges around the state. Life was good and I loved every minute of it.

Our waking hours were filled with family and survival. Having no television, daily newspaper, and radio only when atmospheric conditions were right, we knew little of what went on the world.

There were many chores that needed done before winter set in, but we still had several weeks of late summer left, and we wanted to play. The boys, looking like Huck Finn, rafted the Little Tok River that wound its way through the surrounding countryside. Before it rushed under an old, falling-down bridge it flowed close to our house. The trip totaled seventeen miles, took two days, and allowed our sons an overnight campout.

I had given no thought to our dogs following the boys. Sandy, one of them did. Joe and I didn't know it until after the raft disappeared around a bend and the boys yelled out, "Mom, call Sandy." Engrossed in trying to clamber aboard the raft she took no notice of my voice. I walked to another place close to the river where I thought I could pick her up. She had other plans. I went on to the next spot. She still had other plans.

I called to Mark, "Come to shore. Get her in the raft, then she can go with you." Twenty minutes later, Sandy on board, they pulled away from the bank, and Sandy chose to run around the edge of the raft, promptly capsizing it. She swam to shore. I grabbed her and held her long enough for the boys to get down river and out of sight.

Late the following evening, the boys returned home. They'd had a wonderful trip: caught Grayling, cooked them over an open fire, and camped by themselves for the first time. They told us of the eagle they saw fishing, wolf prints in the sand, moose on the bank, beaver in a pond and, the big fish that got away.

After that trip, feeling like they were old hands at over-nighters, exploring the valleys and hiking the mountains that were their backyard, they frequently camped out.

From the yard in front of our house we watched Dall sheep clambering across ridges. One day we saw forty-two ewes and lambs. Later that same evening a grizzly ambled along one of the many animal trails traversing the mountainsides. There was always something to watch.

A few days later, I climbed with our children and dogs to the top of a four-thousand-foot mountain. We sat and looked across the valley floor dotted with numerous lakes varying in color from jade-green to sapphire-blue, and small streams tumbling to the river below. The taller peaks around us, where snow clung to the shaded areas, probed a cornflower blue sky.

Before we left the mountains, we investigated deserted bird nests, peeked into abandoned dens, followed sheep trails, watched ravens play-fly, shared our picnic with squirrels, picked flowers, and searched for small burls to take home to Joe. As we walked homeward, the sky streaked with orange, lemon yellow, rose pink, and gold as the sun slowly dipped behind the highest peaks.

That same summer, on one of their trips to the mountains, the boys found a complete petrified tree. They carried some home to show us, then decided to take Goldie, the horse we inherited, to help pack more out.

AWAY FROM THE CITY

There's a saying here. "Alaska's only twenty minutes from Anchorage." It's true. A few short miles south of town beside the Seward Highway, Beluga whales torpedo through Cook Inlet, Dall sheep ewes and full-curl rams graze among rocks on the opposite side of the roadway, and coyotes lope along the railroad track.

Away from the city to the north along the Glenn Highway, Sandhill Cranes and Trumpeter swans spend summers on the Hay Flats, while Loons and Grebes pair up on local lakes. Bald eagles and hawks soar on warm thermals above moose browsing on willows. Musk Ox and Caribou roam the tundra, and Polar bears hunt seal and walrus in the Arctic ice fields.

The more distant from the city, the more wildlife is visible.

Where we lived, in a remote area three hundred and fifty miles from Anchorage, for many years, it was not uncommon to see grizzly bears in our yard, fox running through brush, or otters playing on their mud slides. Wolves also traveled through our area.

One winter night, Joe, my husband, and I perched on a rocky ledge in the mountains miles from civilization searching for wolves. The valley below us was bathed in oyster-shell light. A light wind melodically played its way through leafless Birch and Spruce trees with boughs weighted down by snow. Moonbeams shafted through branches, creating whimsical shadows dancing at our feet. Stars twinkled, but Orion held his position far above us.

A three-quarter moon hung behind a curtain of creamy white gossamer veils swaying and swirling across infinity. Reds dissolving into shades of pink shot through with brilliant streaks of green whirled their sinuous way across the dark sky. Joe draped his arm across my shoulders as we sat mesmerized by the display.

A Horned owl arrived on silent wings and landed on a nearby tree. Hunters all, each aware of the other, we waited hoping for a glimpse of what we sought. Minutes stretched to hours. The owl moved on, but we would not give up our search so soon. Our muscles stiff and bones aching from cold, even though we'd bundled up in snowsuits, hats and mitten before buckling on snowshoes to get there. We clapped our cold hands together and shuffled our feet to revive our circulation. My eyes and nose ran from the cold. I wiped them, then sat back down next to Joe.

This was not the first night we had spent seeking wolves. Nor would it be our last. I can't remember a time in my adult life when I wasn't excited by thoughts of them. For me, their lifestyle is the epitome of wildlife. Even those in captivity seem to retain their aloofness and dignity.

On this particular night I knew they were near. I could feel it in my soul. We scanned the ridges, but saw no shapes moving across the moonlit snow. Then I saw them; silhouettes of six wolves snaking along the foothills, moving with purpose in single file. Were they hunting? My heart butted against my ribs. Unaware I'd stopped breathing, I exhaled. My condensed breath floated away like fog into the night. My focus on the pack, I no longer noticed my surroundings or heard the music of the wind.

A howl drifted to us, then another from farther away. What did this communication mean? I hoped it might become apparent if we kept the pack in view.

Across the snow-blanketed landscape, Joe saw and pointed to a moose with her calf. The cow lifted her head then turned her ears to track the howls. Driven by instinct, she trotted deeper into the cover of trees to protect her baby. Her calf followed.

In the suspense filled silence we searched for the pack, but it had vanished. Where were they? What were they doing? With nothing to do but wait, I thought back to other times with other wolves. Over time we had watched them raise young, seen them feed, and spent countless hours following their tracks in mud and snow. A secret desire to understand these animals is what drove me. I needed to personally see the way they lived their life.

The pack that traveled close to our home often spied on us as it circuited through the area. One summer evening, aware of being observed, I looked up and saw five wolves standing statue-still among tree trunks at the edge of our garden. Some winter mornings we found their footprints on a windowsill, where they had rested their front feet while looking in. One especially bold, female black wolf, apparently unconcerned, frequently spent time in plain view eyeballing us when we worked outside. What was she thinking at those times, or when I invaded her territory and spied on her family?

The time passed quickly at first, but with cold seeping into my body it wasn't long before home comforts nudged my mind. A cup of hot coffee to wrap my hands around would be heavenly.

Disappointed that we could not find the wolves again, we stood, stamped our feet and turned to leave. My peripheral vision caught movement. Excited, I zeroed in on dark figures loping along the base of the mountains. Completely absorbed, I watched them leave the foothills and then, with great bounding leaps, cross the valley floor like ghosts.

From a gully to the south, beyond the woods where the moose had entered, five more wolves emerged. Apparently all eleven had worked out their strategy beforehand. The five would chase their prey toward the original six we had been watching. So simple, yet so deadly efficient.

A howl from each group broke the silence. Things were heating up. I felt like an interloper. Should we leave? Did I really want to witness the kill?

Again, the silent hunters disappeared among spruce lined hills. Where were the cow and her calf? Had they managed to put enough distance between themselves and the pack to stay alive? My taut nerves wound even tighter.

Outraged bellows from the moose and rapid yelps

from the wolves answered my questions. In minutes, silence reigned. The chase was over. The pack would survive. The cow would birth again.

We turned homeward. The swishing of our snowshoes accompanied the video playing in my mind of the owl, wolves, moose, and the Aurora.

We had arrived in Alaska more than four decades ago because of our intense interest in wildlife and the wilderness, but we didn't truly find nights like that until we moved away from the city.

A DIFFERENT KIND OF HOBBY

I remember how excited I was the summer I returned to live in Alaska. Standing in awe, I soaked up the view like a dessert when it rains: mountains piercing unblemished blue sky, sapphire and turquoise glaciers, and untainted air. I peered through my camera lens in Anchorage and photographed Mount McKinley over two hundred miles away.

The first moose I saw after I settled into my new home, walked up and seemed to study blazing blooms in my flowerbeds – or was she deciding which ones to eat.

After years of living elsewhere, things were as I remembered. Not much had changed. Anchorage had expanded up the hillside, Wasilla's population had grown, and by the number of cars on the road it seemed that every family must own at least six vehicles, and what they did all day was drive the highway.

When the following spring arrived, the sky filled with birds on their migration route to breeding grounds. Cranes, swans, and geese flying in military V formations called to one another as they flew north. Mother moose with young calves strolled between willows beside the road. Conversations turned to summer fun and evidence of Alaskans gearing up to garden took shape. Owners strapped motorcycles and four-wheelers into pickups, loaded boats on various sized trailers. Bicycles filled racks behind SUVs and motor homes.

Like summers of years past, my garden grew outlandish sized cabbages; some weighing 12 lbs. Rivers and lakes produced trout and salmon the likes of which I'd not seen in my years away. Then in late summer, succulent, red, blue, and salmon pink berries ripened on the hillsides, waiting to be harvested by people and bears. Fuchsia colored Fireweed and rust colored cranberry leaves carpeted the foothills in fall.

In this new-to-me-again world, everything was invigorating and exciting. Winter brought snowcapped pinnacles tinted with the colors of the setting sun, and conditions perfect to snowmobile, ski, sled, and skate. It also brought an opportunity to wear my new down jacket designed to keep me warm while outside on cold days.

Everywhere I turned, old memories stirred anticipation for renewed experiences. For years I had not seen Northern Lights, or watched a dog sled race. Nowhere else had I seen snow carvings, or danced at an event like the Miners and Trappers Ball. In this place, even stars looked close enough to reach up and touch.

Time has not dimmed those feelings. They are with me now as I stand on my back porch and look up at the night sky, or watch wildlife activity in the Game Refuge below the bluff upon which my home is built. However, I have changed with the passing of time. I am no longer as athletically inclined.

Having given up some of the more strenuous forms of recreation, I found I desired a less active hobby to draw me outside, or hold me inside the comfort of my home. I needed to be creative. My friends and I still hike the hills, fish, picnic, and camp out on occasions. I enjoy working in my garden, but flowers have replaced vegetables now, except in my greenhouse where tomatoes, cukes, carrots, beets, and zucchini flourish.

I noticed winters seemed longer and left me feeling a need for something besides a daily walk with my dog, television, writing, and reading. I turned to hobbies of years ago when I painted, created unique candles, and I learned how to burn wildlife designs on burl slabs that sold as clocks and coffee tables. I hooked rugs to hang on the wall or place on the floor. All those things I enjoyed, yet still longed for something new, something different.

The following summer, on a warm sunny day, while visiting with friend on her riverside lawn in Oregon, she said, "Come look at my flowers. They're exceptional this year." As we walked along cobblestone paths weaving their way through spectacular beds of roses, nasturtiums, and pansies and flowering shrubs, I noticed dozens of small ornaments placed in among her floral display. "Oh those," she said. "They're just rocks I found and painted. You should try it.

It's fun." Right then I knew I'd found my new hobby. Painting rocks. Yes. Rocks.

Upon my return home to Alaska, I found myself walking around with my head down, eyes glued to the ground, searching out prospective rocks of various shapes and sizes. My imagination ran wild when I picked up likely possibilities. However, I discovered my imagination far outweighed my abilities. With practice I improved. Then came the day I produced something that at a stretch of the mind could pass as a gnome home. From then on I was truly hooked.

Over time I learned to use wood filler to round off edges, plug unsightly pits, mold chimneys, fashion pillars, cornices, and window frames. With a little effort I found it possible to change an ordinary looking rock into a house, barn, store, church, or an animal. Occasionally, I stumbled onto rocks that didn't need to be reshaped or redesigned. They were perfect, needing only paint to bring them to life.

I enjoy this newfound hobby, and am convinced anyone can do it. You don't need talent, just patience and practice. The supplies needed are minimal: rocks, a good imagination, a few acrylic paints, an assortment of brushes, and varnish to protect your creation from the weather once it is finished and set outside.

I painted a frog on a flat round stone that I now use as a paperweight. It's different. Invariably, when a friend picks it up for a closer look, they are surprised to see legs and cute frog feet painted on the underside. It brings a smile to their face.

If I want something miniature, small flat stones are excellent for painting colorful bugs to set in among houseplants, brighten up a terrarium, or place under a Bonsai tree. They compliment both soil and plant. Out in my yard I have several painted rocks of various shapes and sizes sitting in among my flowers and shrubs: a penguin, several different style houses and cottages, a church and an assortment of animals. They're conversation pieces, an attractive addition to my yard. My daughter and her children paint ladybugs, bears, and beavers, which only goes to prove a person of any age can enjoy this pastime.

Searching for smooth, rounded rocks brought me a day

at the river with a friend. Glacial water rushed by us on its journey to the sea as our dogs worked the bank searching treasures only they could enjoy. My friend and I found jagged rocks beside unpaved roads carved along a hillside. The edges of a highway or a driveway are other places that produced a wide variety of shapes and sizes. Another good source, if you can get permission, are gravel pits where every size rock imaginable is available. Painting on gravel does make a nice miniature to compliment a Bonsai.

If this hobby sounds intriguing, there are books available by Lin Wellford to help with this particular kind of craft. They are full of instructions on how to turn an ordinary rock into a work of art. Her books contain pages of wonderful ideas and an abundance of color photos that show each step of the procedure.

RESTLESS SPIRITS

About a mile from our house one full moon winter night, Kodiak, my dog, and I entered a favorite grove. There in the diminished light, intermingled with the soughing wind, the sound of frozen branches scraping against each other, and the crunch of my footsteps was the whispering and giggling of two children. Surprised, I stopped. Kodiak tilted his head to one side as though listening, while questions tumbled through my brain. Who are those children? What are they doing there at this time of night? Why are they not home in bed? Where are their parents?

Curious, I moved toward the center of the grove. Kodiak followed. The childish sounds grew louder. I watched as shadowed shapes drifted back and forth then vanished into darkness too dense to penetrate. The whispering and giggling slowly faded. Now I felt unsure if they had been real.

Mind running in high gear, nerves spiked, my thoughts turned to the story I'd heard of lives ended violently or too soon, leaving their souls lingering in limbo. Now I wondered, could those children have been specters, wraiths, or unsettled little souls? Standing there mystified, Shakespeare's words spoken by Hamlet echoed in my head, "There are more things in heaven and earth, Horatio, than are dreamt of in your philosophy."

Kodiak, ears pricked to gather sound, eyes searching, nostrils expanding and contracting, inhaled information in the night air. From his demeanor, it appeared he was undisturbed by what I had seen and heard.

Sometime later, we entered an open area outside the grove, where moonlight washed the surrounding countryside. I looked back. Only spruce limbs dusted with snow swayed and cast shadows on the ground. The breeze continued to sigh.

We trekked to the edge of a pond and stopped. I noticed the feathery designs in the moonlit, wind-polished ice. Kodiak scanned the area. Suddenly, with feet planted firmly, a plaintive whimper escaped from somewhere deep inside him. "What is it, boy?" Holding my breath, I listened. Nothing. Then a wolf howl erupted.

In the quiet that followed, I scrutinized the place where Kodiak gazed intently. My eyes zeroed in on what appeared to be wolf standing at the edge of another pond not far away. "Is that one of your ancestors, boy?" I said, ruffling the hair between Kodiak's ears. Suddenly, whatever it was disappeared into deeper shadows along the bank. Weaker, much weaker, another howl reached my ears.

Dark clouds gathered on the horizon, rolled quickly across the sky and slipped in front of the moon, filling me with a sudden unexpected sense of dread. "Come on, boy. We better go."

About two thirds of the way home on the old, dirt road, the moon no longer hidden, shone bright once again. Kodiak stopped, blocking my path. Seconds later he moved to our right, off the trail and into a stand of naked birch. A few yards farther in his steps slowed. "What's the matter, boy?" Then I saw it. A dead wolf partially covered by a recent snowfall. Brushing snow away, I saw the female had been shot. Kodiak whined, then looked into my eyes. "I know, fella." I said. "I'm sorry." Gathering fallen twigs and leaves to cover her, I thought how sad it was her life had been extinguished and her body just left. Even the trees looked dejected.

The next morning, sitting at the kitchen table, mulling over the events of the previous night, I decided to find out if anything untoward had happened in that grove.

Later, when a suspect was arrested, the story resurfaced about two murdered children, a brother and sister, their bodies found in a shallow grave near the center of our favorite grove. Apparently, busy with life at the time of the tragedy the story slipped by me unnoticed.

After reading about them, I wondered if their souls had been what I saw and heard, or had my imagination been running in overdrive? I prefer to believe it was real. The thought of those children giggling and playing for eternity after the way their young lives ended so tragically sits well in my mind.

Later, my thoughts turned to the wolf at the pond, and I now questioned if that had been real. "Kodiak," I said. "What do you think? Could it have been the spirit of the dead wolf we found?" I pushed out of the chair, walked to the counter to pour coffee. Turning, cup in hand, I noticed him watching me. "Oh, fella," I said. "If only you could speak, you could tell me the answer. I know you know."

THE PREDATOR

The incoming clouds piled up and overwhelmed the sun. The shadows, in their private places under the trees decorated with red, orange, and yellow leaves, stopped dancing and disappeared. Until the storm moved closer, the forest dwellers took little notice of the distant rumble of thunder and lightening that zipped across the sky. The sporadic rain changed to a downpour, and unrest coursed its jagged way from animal to animal. Something was threatening their world.

A lynx, the mother of four, recognized disaster in a squirrel racing across a clearing carrying a baby in her mouth, and a Hawk owl, a bird of the night, making its silent escape above the forest. The owl, intent on flight, did not seek out the squirrel, and the squirrel paid the owl no heed. A rain-drenched hare dragged itself through the sludge where rain and hail had pounded the ground to a muddy quagmire.

Claps of thunder, closer now and louder, frightened the lynx kittens. As lightning zigzagged through the gun-metal-gray sky they shook with fear. The small family moved to the shelter of a hollow log. A crack as loud as a rifle shot reverberated around them when forked-lightening struck the outstretched arm on a dead tree. More scared now, the kittens leaned into their mother, clambered over her as she crouched in their small sanctuary. Thunder roared overhead, resonated through the forest and quivered ground beneath their feet.

In passing, the storm left behind a tiny flame at the base of the struck tree, which grew into a monster out of control; a fiendish predatory offspring to stalk the forest and gorge itself on trees, brush, and wildlings. The fire created its own wind. Drove flames in ever-widening circles. Lay waste to everything in its path.

It followed the contours of the land. Jumped water barriers with the ease of frogs leaping from lily pad to lily pad. Bypassing wet swampy ground it leapt from treetop to treetop spewing its malignancy back to earth. Exploding trees added to the terror of the lynx family. Aspen, birch, and spruce flared and lent fury to the holocaust. Heaving clouds of steam mixed with suffocating smoke, some trees toppled into shallow pools.

Foreboding filled the air. The mother lynx tensed as eye-watering smoke burst into her valley. Choking panic seized her. As the frantic need to flee channeled its way through her, she summoned her kits to her side.

While the roaring inferno galloped across the valley floor, the obscene predator belched gray breath that filtered through the forest, maiming and killing without discretion. Its groping fingers reached out to engulf nearby bushes. Heat crinkled their leaves, curled their bark. Flames gobbled them up. Tongues of fire licked indiscriminately at tiny plants, shrubs, moss, and delicate flowering roses, which shriveled and died before being engulfed by the intruder. A glutton, the predator grew larger by the minute.

The lynx family sped to a pond. Finding it edged by fire they turned and dashed toward the river. Racing between burning trees, lungs aching as though filled with sand, nostrils burning from acrid fumes in the smoke-filled air, they fled across the hot scorched earth. Fireballs plunged from above as animals dodged their desperate way, seeking safety. One young lynx misjudged falling debris. A small flaming bough settled on his back. A strangled cry escaped as his coat smoldered, then burst into flames that seared his flesh. Heart thumping loudly in his ears, cold fear pushed him on. His pain increased until, unable to keep pace, he lost sight of his family. His hearing faded, his vision blurred, his strength failed. He lay dying amid the destruction.

On invisible legs, the predator cleared creeks to continue its rampage on the opposite side. Cranberry bushes shooting flames at their nearest neighbors dropped suddenly cremated berries. Brush erupted into volcanoes shooting ash and red-hot sparks. Puffs of gray flew into the air as large raindrops punched tiny holes into layers of ash covering the forest floor. Fueled by resin-filled conifers, oily black smoke rose in thick columns, turning day into dusk.

Not to be denied an identity at its most destructive moments, the fire created a face of evil in brilliant reds and oranges, with gray and black shadows forming horns, eyes, snout, and a mouth. A Raging Red Bull Mask, so distinguishable by its features it demanded recognition. All Nature cringed.

Seeking escape, panicked birds flew above the canopy. Red Voles frantically shifted their small families from place to place, and terrorized squirrels continued to seek safety. Foam bubbled at the ends of decaying moss-covered logs. Squeals of pain and terror intermingled with the sound of snapping branches, crackling undergrowth, roaring flames, and exploding trees.

Evergreens, hundreds of years old, shed seed-filled cones and dropped sacrificial needles into the pyre. Thick golden, sticky sap dribbled its way down deep furrows in tree bark to join the crisped foliage below. Even roots buried beneath the forest floor could not survive the onslaught. Rain could not drown the intruder.

Moose, the quiet travelers of the forest, crashed mindlessly through trees and brush in terror. Like all the animals they had but one purpose, to escape the burning doom. No birds could be heard. They were gone, flown away. Only the unfledged remained in their nests while the fiery trees consumed them. Wildlings fled, putting distance between themselves and the fury that threatened their lives. Relationships forgotten, foe and friend raced along trails side by side. Voices of the too young, too old, too weak, too inexperienced, echoed through the land.

Trampled beneath the feet of fleeing animals, another young lynx succumbed, but the mother, relentless in her search for safety, did not stop. Driven by instinct, she herded her remaining family toward the safety of water.

Wildlings lay gasping and dying while others, like her, mindless of blistered, cracked and bleeding feet, fled on to the river. Once there, they leapt into the water to join the many animals already huddled between its banks. All struggled against the strong current. Some, including a lynx kitten, were washed away. Bristles gone, skin charred, a porcupine along with other bodies burned beyond recognition floated by them; victims of the land that was once their home. Sizzling embers settled on the banks, while flying sparks hissed and died on the water's surface.

Once the firestorm moved beyond them, the mother lynx and her one remaining offspring dragged their bodies onto the riverbank. She shook herself then licked her youngster dry. They and other survivors of the onslaught returned to their homes amid the devastation. The stench of scorched feathers, flesh, and smoldering timber assaulted them.

Wildlife hid in the mosaic pattern of charred skeletal remains of trees and brush. Animals severely injured became easy prey. A crippled moose fell victim to wolves, a seared hare to the owl; a homeless squirrel fed the hawk, and a blinded fox became a meal for the lynx and her young one.

With the next spring rains, layers of ash provided nutrients for new growth.

RADIOSONDE

Winter seemed to be the time of year when special occurrences took place. That year, Joe had been out on snowshoes and seen something hanging from a tree branch. It was a Radiosonde, an instrument the Weather Bureau uses to collect data. Once he arrived home, we checked it out and found a tag attached to it that said, "Return to address below. State time and location found." We wrote a letter to accompany the tag. Our only hope was the employees at the ESSA Illinois Station had a sense of humor.

Dear Sir.

We located this Radiosonde one half mile south of the Chena Hot Springs Road, twenty-five miles N E of Fairbanks, Alaska.

On that particular day, at the exact point of landing, a rather ill tempered moose was lying under the tree in which the parachute landed, taking a badly needed nap after trudging through four feet of snow for many days. The landing of your Radiosonde disturbed him to the point of becoming neurotic.

In his neurotic state he pawed the ground, which upset the rabbit population and caused them to stampede. Of course, that upset the moose even more. Mass confusion set in: rabbits stampeded, squirrels chattered, lynx spat and hissed, fox yelped, snowbirds fluttered, and wolves howled. To get away from this the moose started running, gathering speed. Due to his speed and the fact his head was down, his vision was impaired and he didn't see our house. When he hit the side, the roof caved in, doors fell off hinges, light fixtures were jarred loose, windows broke, cabinets dropped from walls and, naturally, broke all our dishes.

Enclosed is an itemized bill in the amount of $30,000.00 for damages. This can be paid in a lump sum or installments at the low monthly rate of $50.00, with no interest.

Yours truly????

ITEMIZED STATEMENT OF EXPENDITURES
Veterinarian fee$1,000.00
Tranquilizers for moose$20.00
Tranquilizers for family$45.00
New roof$3,000.00 (shingles instead of dirt)
Fill hole in wall$100.00 (old rags)
Fill hole in other wall$100.00 (more old rags.)
Replace windows$400.00 (glass instead of plastic)
Re-hang doors$40.00 (new hinges.)
Replace door jams$200.00
Build cabinets$1,500.00 (replaced original orange crates.)
Oil furnace$700.00 (replaced pot-bellied stove.)
Set of china$250.00 (replaced tin plates.)
New suit for husband$200.00 (replaced torn jeans while retrieving Radiosonde.)
Fine paid to Fur, Fish, and Game$22,440.00 (shooting moose out of season.)
Typing fee$5.00
Sub-total$30,000.00
Less25.00 (Received from pawn shop for Radiosonde)TOTAL DUE $29,975.00

This is the answer we received from Mr. Rahmlow in Arlington Virginia.

Dear Mr. and Mrs. Johannes.

We have been receiving reports from Radiosonde finders for over thirty years, but until your letter arrived, I did not realize the full potential of such a small instrument.

As an ex-forester ranger, I can understand the capability of disturbed animals breaking all your tin dishes. It is equally heartbreaking to have a dirt roof disturbed. "Be it ever so humble, there's no place like home." You probably are still experiencing chills and drafts caused by the rags shrinking after they became wet. The enclosed description of the Radiosonde observations is being provided to enable you to start papering your new walls.

After having prepared your Income Tax report, you undoubtedly realize how difficult it is to give money to the government. Let me assure you that it's almost as difficult to collect money! If you will forward a certified receipt from the F and G Department, certified copies of the invoices covering construction material, and the tin cups from your old set of dishes, we'll start a collection to meet the $50.00 monthly payments.

We assume the item of $20.00 for tranquilizers was a "bar bill" to insure the moose would die happy, and the $1,000.00 veterinarian fee was incurred after he was shot.

We greatly appreciate your efforts in returning the Radiosonde. In the future we will have the winds blow in another direction to avoid disturbing the tranquility of Chena Hot Springs Road.

Sincerely yours, …

Our oldest son, Mark, found another Radiosonde later in that same winter. By that time Mr. Rahmlow had retired so we sent this Christmas letter to his replacement.

Dear Sir.

We appreciate the fact that you are not responsible for promises made by your predecessor, but feel you should know he did promise to "have the winds blow in a different direction so as not to disturb our tranquility. As you can see by the tag enclosed, that promise has been broken.

This Radiosonde did not create the same amount of disturbance as the previous one. However, it did disrupt our resident Great Horned Owl. He now sits in his favorite tree saying, "Heee. Heeee," instead of "Hooooo. Hooooooooo!"

Alaska isn't too bad if you don't mind a few inconveniences like Radiosondes dropping out of a clear blue sky. The winter months are quite dark and snow filled, but at least the snow fills some of the cracks in the cabin walls and keeps out some of the cold.

Several days ago I went out to find the dogs, but the wind came up quite unexpectedly, so by the time I found my way back to the cabin one of my ears was frozen. Thank goodness we had had some first aid training. Even though it was a new experience for him, Joe did quite well with a hatchet.

When we first came here years ago, this place had plenty of trees. However, after a while it has become necessary to go further a-field for our wood. Last week I managed to get some close to the cabin. A moose had run into the outhouse, so we burned it --- the outhouse, not the moose. I suppose it will have to be fed from now until spring when the ice thaws and it can get out.

Going out to get the mail isn't too bad. The three mile trek doesn't usually take long, even on snowshoes when there is a wolf not far behind. Less when there are two or three.

We really don't anticipate many problems from our resident bear and her cub this year, even though they have hibernated in the basement. However, their snoring does tend to keep us awake at night. Needless to say when the mother porcupine had her babies in our bed it did cause some spine tingling moments. The squirrel that moved into the children's closet made it necessary for us to buy all new underwear for them.

Most of our time our life is uneventful. I still have the same three children and six grandchildren, even though I tried to lose them a couple of times. The bears kept bringing them back! The salmon we smoked turned out well. At least we must assume it did. The bears ate it all.

As you most probably know, a garden grows well in Alaska. This year the moose ate most of it, but we are now eating moose. The melons didn't do as well as we had hoped. The vines grew so quickly they drug the melons across the ground and wore them down to the size of gherkins.

The Caribou migrated early this year. We could tell by the hoof prints in our living room sod floor.

One of the neighbors stopped by. Can't remember her name. You wouldn't think a person would forget so quickly. It has only been three years since I saw her. Any way, she said it was rumored that a man called Clinton was president. What happened to Truman?

Since the ptarmigan nested in the gramophone we no longer can listen to our favorite songs, "North to Alaska" and "Springtime in Alaska", but that's all right.

With the New Year coming up we have made some resolutions:

(1) Build concrete outhouse.

(2) Soundproof basement.

(3) Remove melon vines from neighbor's house.

(4) Remove Wolverine from mailbox. (Mailman refuses to deliver mail until we do.)

(5) Find new route to mailbox

(6) Anchor dogs to trees so mosquitoes will not carry any more of them off this coming spring.

I must close now. The dogs are hitched to their sled, and I am off to the trading post for some Christmas supplies. Have a wonderful New Year, and do try to do better about changing the wind direction.

The Radiosonde Retriever Club.

The Johannes Family

We never heard from ESSA again and could only assume Mr. Rahmlow's replacement had less sense of humor.

THE GOSHAWK I WANTED TO KILL

Infrequently, owls and hawks caused us problems by ravaging our poultry. One large Goshawk, which moved into our area, seemed to have one aim in life – to devastate our turkey poult population. One morning, about 4.30 A.M., he succeeded in annihilating several of them. The chaotic noise woke me. Abandoning my bed, I rushed outside.

The remaining live poults were beside themselves with terror, running in circles and screeching at him as he stood tearing apart their family members. Some of them, so freaked, were lying unconscious.

When the hawk noticed me, he glared at me then flew off with a half-eaten bird in his talons. I couldn't help it; all I wanted to do was destroy him like he'd done to my baby birds. I raced to the house and grabbed a gun with intention of hunting him down.

He perched in a tree close to the house. Talons extended, he swooped at me as I ran out the door. His feet brushed through my hair, removing some by its roots as he flew by. Now I was determined to annihilate him.

He landed on a stump not far away. Off I went, resolved to destroy him. As I closed in, he flew again. I followed. Three hours later, we had covered many acres. Tromping after him, I had time to cool off and collect my thoughts. What was the matter with me? I had never killed and I couldn't kill now, but I wanted him to know I didn't like him or approve of his behavior – even it was his natural way.

He settled in a tree. Knowing I couldn't hit him from where I stood, I raised the gun and fired one defiant shot. Feeling somewhat vindicated, I returned to the remaining turkeys to settle them down and clean up the mess.

The parent turkeys lived in a separate pen, and because of their size we never concerned ourselves with their safety from birds of prey. We knew there wasn't a hawk around big enough to haul them off, but we had not considered eagles. We should have. After all, I knew they could carry off a fox kit and Dall sheep lambs.

Tom, our biggest breeding male turkey, strutting his stuff for his harem, was oblivious to the Golden Eagle plummeting toward him. In the battle that ensued Tom lost. The eagle tried to lift off with the twenty-eight-pound turkey in his talons, but Tom's weight proved too much. Damaged beyond any help we could give, Joe was forced to kill Tom.

Later in the day, the family decided I needed a break away from the darker side of life. I packed a picnic. At the pond where we ate, we watched a cow moose ducking her head under water to reach succulent plants growing in the mud bottom. Her calf stood on the bank watching its mother as ever-widening circles broke the smooth surface. When the ripples reached a beaver lodge in the middle of the dam, the mother beaver surfaced to investigate. Finding nothing threatening, she swam to shore to collect leafy willows to take to her young.

Families of ducks swam in and out of the reeds growing on the opposite shore. Trying not to be seen by the ever-watchful beaver, Kodiak, my dog, eased along the edge, disturbing White Sox, clouds of mosquitoes and gnats hidden in the grass. The ever-aware beaver saw him and slapped his tail on the surface to alert its family to danger.

A mother Mallard close to shore, acting as though injured, swam a short distance away. Kodiak jumped in the midst of the small family. The mother duck skimmed across the surface, quacking all the way, hoping to attract his attention. Once on shore, she dragged her wing and limped away. Kodiak followed. Apparently satisfied her brood was safe, the mother suddenly rose into the air. The moose, which had watched the commotion, lowered her ears, and stepped in Kodiak's direction. Threatened, he sped away.

On the way home we stopped to watch a fox bathing in the river. Her tail trailed behind her in the current. Eyes, barely slits, and head out of the cool water she slowly floated downstream. When she noticed us, she leapt to the bank, shook, and then raced away.

Our children loved our way of life, which was not unlike my own childhood. I watched our daughter dress goslings as I had done at her age. She placed bonnets on their head; scarves around their neck then took them for a wheelbarrow ride. The boys, caring and kind, had a more practical attitude concerning our livestock; they killed chickens, and the Thanksgiving turkey, telling their sister, "We raised them to eat, didn't we?" Upset, she called them "Murderers." However, when Joe served a roasted bird, she filled her plate.

PUFF

One evening, Puff, our daughter Janny's poodle, disappeared. Not normally far away, it was unusual for him not to come when Janny called. We searched everywhere we could think of but couldn't find him.

"Try not to worry, Sweetheart. He'll be back," Joe told Janny, who was almost in tears because she thought some terrible fate had befallen Puff.

Puff wandered, but usually only a short distance into the trees that edged our lawn. He had set limits to his territory; knew where he belonged and didn't stray.

None of us really believed Joe's words. Dread took the place of anxiety, but still I nodded our agreement. While I fixed dinner, a picture flashed across my mind of Puff struggling to get out of some mud. The place looked familiar, but I couldn't pinpoint it at that moment. Then suddenly it came to me. I rushed out of the house, ran along the garden fence to a spot near some spruce trees. There he was, just as I'd visualized him. I raced back to the house to get Joe and our kids. Puff needed our help.

Puff had started making his way across an area of quicksand. Now it was swallowing him. We couldn't reach him. The boys sped off then returned with a wide plank. Joe started across it. His weight caused it to sink. I tried, with the same results. Finally, Scott lay on his stomach and wriggled toward a pathetically whimpering Puff.

By the time Scott reached him, Puff had sunk another couple of inches. Scott tried to pull him out. Puff screeched in pain. The sand was crushing his small body as it dragged him down. Scott had no choice. He yanked on the little dog until he freed him. Janny leaned into Joe, crying. Tears brimmed my eyes. Joe put his arm around me, while Mark tried to console his sister.

As soon as we had Puff in the house, I ran a tub of warm water in which to place his mud-caked, quivering body. He never fully recovered from the experience; his spine had been damaged. The veterinarian could not help him. He lived the remainder of his life with his head tilted to one side.

Before retiring that night, I made my usual check on our kids. I covered the boys with blankets they had kicked off in their sleep, and then walked to Janny's room. She and Puff were snuggled close, both with their head on the same pillow. I bent down, kissed them then said a "Thank you, Lord" prayer before I crawled into my own bed.

Held prisoner by sand, Puff's experience not only left its mark on his mind, it also affected his body. After that experience, he refused to be parted from Janny and, always underfoot, made sure she stayed within his sight.

A MOOSE HUNT

Moose hunting season is a beautiful time of year, with bright sunny days, leaves changing from green to gold, and clear, crispy nights. Whenever possible, we hunted as a family. Both Mark, and Scott, our sons, had shot their moose; Mark was twelve years old when he first provided meat for that particular winter. A couple of years later it was Scott's turn. Janny, our daughter, nor I actually hunted in the sense of shooting animals, but we did a lot of bird-dogging for the men in our family.

There were those times that only Joe, my husband, and I hunted. We drove or walked many miles searching out our quarry, and saw so much wildlife on those trips. As we crossed dams we often saw beaver lazily swimming across their pond or busily dragging a branch with leaves still attached to eat under the ice when the pond was frozen over. Ptarmigan fluttered short distances between the trees, a lone raven followed overhead, cawing as it flew.

Sometimes we caught a glimpse of a fox running across the trail. Small chickadees flitted in and out branches, squirrels chattered and scolded, ermine undulated through the downed leaves looking for mice and voles.

One old raven that lived close to the house for years, often followed our truck as we drove old logging roads. He had observed several of our hunting forays, patiently waiting on a nearby limb for us to finish up so he could be the first to pick through leftovers. He was there on this particular trip when we went for our 'looking for a moose' ride.

Joe and I had jumped in the truck, headed for a slough a few miles from our house, not really expecting to see anything except moose prints, but always hopeful. We drove a long time seeing nothing that even looked promising. Then, deciding to call it a day and turn homeward, Joe said, "Oh well, maybe next time". Suddenly, we saw something, a dark shape close to the edge of a pond. It was dusk by then, so we were not sure if it was a moose, but because we were so familiar with the area we knew it was not a bush, a mound of dirt, or anything that was usually in that particular spot. I stopped; Joe reached for his gun to look through the scope. In the dimming light he saw it was a moose. Now we knew for sure, we had to decide if he should shoot it or not. After all, it was standing on the bank close to the water, and we had heard many horror stories about situations just like that.

Joe decided to wait for the moose to turn to be sure it would run further along the bank away from the water, if it ran at all. We waited for what seemed like hours, but in reality it was only minutes.

Joe kept watch of the bull through the scope on his 7mm rifle. Standing beside him, my mind in turmoil, switched from, "Joe, don't miss, we need the meat." to, "Joe, don't kill him". The moose turned. Joe squeezed the trigger. The sound shattered the quiet. The bull spun around. Took about a dozen steps. Then dropped dead in the water; and sank out of sight. Neither of us said a word. We simple watched as the water settled back to a clear, calm, surface. In a matter of seconds the whole area looked as though nothing had happened, except for the two of us standing there with our mouths open.

Not speaking, we turned; climbed into the truck, returned home to collect the gear we needed for the night's work ahead. Number one on the list was the canoe. Then came paddles, ropes, and knives. I strapped on my Smith and Wesson 357 pistol incase we needed to impress on any wolves or bears that the bull was ours. We tucked the children in bed, kissed them, said, "Good night," told them, "Don't worry, we'll be home as soon as possible," and then left.

Our return journey to the slough was mostly in silence. Both of us contemplated how we could best accomplish the task ahead. Once at the slough, we put the canoe in what we thought was water but found it to be ice. Well, ice or not, we must to get that moose. Off we paddled, breaking ice all the way. During what little conversation we had during the crossing, we named our canoe "Mini Manhattan", after a real icebreaker, and concluded we would not like to spend our lives in that particular profession.

By then the almost full moon was up, but it was not yet a

bright, moonlit night. We were glad of the light, but the area had an eerie appearance. Trees stood stark and skeletal. A breeze whispered its way through their branches. Shadows on the ground moved silently in their macabre little dance.

Once we reached the moose, we noticed we were about fifteen feet from the bank on the other side, and only five feet from a small island. With the rope under water, Joe proceeded to tie the hind legs of the moose. He then attached the rope to the canoe. From my previous experience of falling into icy water, I could imagine how his hands must hurt. The pinging pain in finger nails, the ache in the knuckles, and a stiffness that made everything awkward.

I heard growling and grumbling coming from the island and asked, in as normal a voice as I could muster, "Joe, what was that?" "Nothing. Just my stomach!" he mumbled as he turned his head away from me.

With the bull's legs tightly secured, we started our journey back to the other bank. Unless you have paddled a canoe through ice, with a thousand pound weight dragging along behind you, you will never know how we puffed, huffed, struggled, and strained. All my romantic visions of gliding across a moonlit lake with a handsome man at the helm disappeared with the crackling, tinkling sound of breaking ice, and our grunts and groans as we used the paddles like punting poles to inch our way across.

As we climbed onto the bank Joe said, "The worst is over. All we have to do now is back the truck up, hook the towrope to the animal and pull it out of the water and up onto the bank. "Wrong! It did not work out to be quite that simple. Three times that moose came half way out of the water. Each time, the rope broke letting our treasure slip down under the icy water. On the fourth try the truck slid, got stuck, and spun half-turns in the road when it hit the end of the rope. The bed of the truck bent. That moose was large but I swear it got bigger as time slipped by! Once it finally was out, it was so unexpected we dragged it into the middle of the road! At least it was on dry land. We felt the tension let up then took a moment to congratulate ourselves.

We retrieved Joe's favorite hunting knife. The one he had previously sharpened to hold an edge through the whole process. We set out plastic bags for the heart and liver, then unloaded the chain saw and a sack of rags to wipe our hands on when through butchering.

First, we opened up the stomach. Steam drifted into the night air. The warmth felt good on our cold hands, but the odor of guts and blood hung heavy in our nostrils. After removing the liver and heart we placed them in the bags. Next, we removed the hindquarters. Joe then chainsawed off the hooves and the part of the leg that had no useable meat.

With the hindquarters separated, we intended to simply throw them into the truck; we could hardly lift them! They weighed about 200 lbs each. Next came the front quarters and neck, which meant removing the head. The rib cage we left in tact and last, but not least, the head with its sixty-one inch antlers.

All the time we worked a 'something' had been patiently waiting for us to get done so it could get to the leftovers. Several times we heard whatever it was change positions. We hoped its patience would not give out before we were finished!

With everything in the truck, all that remained was to retrieve the canoe. We walked down the bank to pull it out of the water only to find it was solidly frozen in place. At that point it didn't seem to matter after all we'd been through; we were just grateful to be done.

We headed home feeling weary and content knowing we now had meat for the winter. Joe and the boys would still hunt for a sheep and game birds. That meat along with salmon, pike, halibut, and huge selection of vegetables from our acre garden would provide some fine fare for the coming year.

We parked the truck in front of the house. Our children were getting up. They quickly grabbed shoes, threw coats over their pajamas, rushed out to see our moose. With a quick, "Hi," they raced passed us and climbed into the bed of the truck. Joe, with his arm over my shoulder, and I walked to the house. We left the children, "Oohing" and "Aahing." When they came in, they had decided they wanted moose steak and eggs for breakfast.. I told them, "First things first. Your Dad and I need dry clothes, and hot coffee."

After changing in to sweats, and downing a cup of hot coffee, Joe returned to the truck, sharp knife in hand. Working together, we manhandled the meat, carried it into the garage to hang from rafters. Then Joe cut off some steaks. Janny collected eggs from the barn, brought them to the stove, where a large pan sizzled with steaks and sliced onions. The kitchen was alive with activity, and mouthwatering aromas.

After breakfast, I filled the tub with hot water for Joe to soak his weary body, while I cleared away the dishes and straightened up the kitchen. He told me, "At first the hot water was painful to ease into, but soon the warmth took over." Sounds of obvious enjoyed comfort emanated from the bathroom. Later, when I took warmed towels in for him to use, I found him with his eyes tightly shut, mouth open, and sound asleep.

Our garage had no door. The meat hung in there for a week. All the time it was there we worried hungry critters might come to eat on it. Every morning animal tracks showed in the dirt driveway. Each night our dogs sat barking and growling warnings to whatever it was that threatened to venture too close.

Cutting up that moose for the freezer was no small task. To begin with, each section had to be stripped of the hide then brought to the kitchen table. Knives needed resharpened, various sacks set aside for the different cuts of meat, a grinder readied for use, freezer paper cut to size, tape, markers, cloths for the occasional hair that stubbornly clung to the meat, and a box for bones.

Three days later, Joe and boys plunked the final 200-pound hindquarter on the table. Usually it took us two long evenings to complete an entire moose, which included grinding approximately 300 pounds of burger. A moose that size provided us with about 600 pounds of meat. An impressive, welcome sight just as winter settled in. As a younger man, Joe was a journeyman butcher so he made sure we all did our part as professionally as possible. He taught us well.

A week later, the family we returned to where we first gutted the moose. We wanted to see if the remains had been eaten. The immediate surrounding area was covered with bear and wolf tracks, as well as several fox, mink and ermine. Raven prints were the most prevalent. A few well-gnawed bones lay about, the marrow licked out of them as far as a tongue could reach. Standing there with frost on our eyelashes and ice in our nostrils, we rehashed our experience, and decided we'd do it again. However, we could never recommend anyone make a practice of marinating whole moose in ice water.

Even when that particular moose was cut, wrapped, and in the freezer, it was not quite over for Joe. His birthday was two days away. The children made his cake. I decorated it with a moose sitting on a creek bank, head in hooves, its' "elbows" on its "knees" saying, "What do you mean he sank!!"

First thing the next morning, our children ran into our bedroom shouting, "Hey Dad. We've got another moose to cut up!" With a heavy groan their father stumbled out of bed, wandered to the kitchen to see what all the commotion was about. A big smile spread across his face when he realized all he had to do was cut his cake.

THE GYRFALCON

The rain stopped. The air held a delicate aroma of wet spruce. Summer, with lush undergrowth, roses, and numerous wild flowers was drifting into fall. We still had time before moose season for one or two more trips to the rivers and creeks filled with salmon and grayling, which were plentiful in their shaded hiding places along the water's edge.

We left the house hours before dusk. A cross fox darted across the trail in front of us. We saw a small flock of grouse scratching in search of food beneath a spruce tree. Always eager to fish, our children ran ahead. As Joe and I walked, he talked about predator/prey relationships, acknowledging himself as a predator. I knew he admired prey animals, considered them highly complex beings, not just food. He showed them respect, and killed only to feed us, or if a critter was suffering and beyond help, and to protect his family.

As we strolled along, a large Gyrfalcon, gliding on the wind, caught our attention as it rose higher and higher into a china-blue sky. Suddenly, with wings folded, the bird plunged earthward at what appeared to be devastating speed. Then, with only a few feet to spare, opened its wings and skimmed over the tall grasses, then rose with a squirrel grasped in its talons. Landing on the highest branch of the tallest tree the hawk devoured its meal then preened its feathers.

A few weeks later, the temperature dropped and a cold wind blew across the valley, sending the remaining rust and yellow colored leaves from the boughs. The first skiff of ice formed on ponds behind beaver dams. Bull moose fought exhausting battles for the right to breed. The sound of mating calls and antlers colliding drifted to us. In the cold, gloomy hours before daylight, the last stragglers of Canada geese flying south passed over. Not far behind them, higher in the sky, lingering swans.

Soon after that the first powdery flakes of snow drifted to earth, transforming our world to pristine beauty and muted sounds. Winter's harshness swept down from the mountains, and with it brought hunger and death to some animals and birds. On occasions we found Chickadees frozen like popsicles, their threadlike feet still wrapped around a branch. Owls and hawks, predators from on high searching for an easy meal, raided traps not yet set off, and were then prey for passing fox or lynx. Sometimes trappers found birds alive, which they delivered to us. We had three Great Horned owls, a goshawk, and an eagle, all with frozen feet. By early summer the birds healed and were released back to the wilds.

THE LAND REMEMBERS

While growing, up my father told me, "The land remembers. That's one of the reasons you feel so content when you come home." At that time, I thought it was another of his Irish tales, but after leaving my parents farm I realized he was right. No matter what happened or where life carried me, the sense of quiet comfort upon returning to the place of my childhood was always there.

For me, "The Land" is the farm of my youth. That land remembers me as the child who played hide and seek in the old, wooden barn, and the red brick cowshed; the small person who suffered through measles, walked to school with friends, and was thrilled at the prospects of a gift from the Tooth Fairy; family dinners after sitting between my parents on Sundays in the eleventh century church where nothing ever changed, and the days I rode my horse down in the copse to a little stream to sit and watch minnows streaking through shafts of sunlight piercing the water. The hedged fields where pheasants hid, and I played in with my dog, and the time, as a teenager, in the hayloft when tears rolled freely with the pain of my first broken heart.

Now an adult, like my father who maintained we leave part of ourselves, which some call our Aura, my beliefs are like his. Here in my home there are certain places I automatically turn to, a particular chair or one end of the couch. Not because it's convenient but because they feel right. They are my comfort zones. Though there are four chairs to choose from at the dining room table, only one draws me. After sharing time on a first visit to a friend's house, I find that invisible force pulling me to the same chair in their home.

We all have those places where we feel most comfortable; be it the land of our youth, a small apartment, or a favorite fishing hole we frequent. I am convinced they all remember.

WILEY COYOTE

We found a coyote den at the base of the mountains not far from our home. Over the years we never saw pups, only adults. The first time we saw them was on an early summer day. They were running along the side of a road then veered off into the bushes before we drew close. The next time we saw them it was up close and personal; they were stalking our poultry pen, and sniffing around our daughter's rabbit cages. Frequent visitors over time, we named them Mr. and Mrs. Wiley.

During winters their prints in the snow gave them away. In summers the dusty ground showed their tracks. The dogs, Sandy, and Kodiak, disliked them, and gave chase at every opportunity. They never stood a chance against the coyote's wily ways, however.

Our son, Mark, at fifteen and his younger brother, Scott, thirteen, wanted to trap the coyotes, but we wouldn't allow them to trap close to our house, but they did trap a distance away from home during the years we lived in the bush. We set stringent rules they must abide by; checking their line every day regardless of the weather, skin the caught animals, stretch them on boards, and arrange for the sale of pelts. They were proficient and dedicated.

Learning responsibility was a big part of our children's growing up. As youngsters, they all had pets; cats, dogs, rabbits, a hamster they sometimes needed to be reminded to feed and water, and guinea pigs. We insisted they treat them with respect, and to understand that animals have feeling. We were adamant they cared for them.

My first upset over trapping started one day while Joe and I were driving home. It was wintertime; the ground was covered with snow. I saw people-tracks in the snow, other than those belonging to our family. We decided to follow them because they were in the confines of our son's trapping area. At a well-trampled area, the moment I opened the truck door, I heard a sound not distinguishable until I heard it a second time. I ran to look down the bank, willing it to be something other that what I felt sure was there.

Desperate, the trapped coyote was trying to get away from the jaws clamped on its front leg. I spoke to him; he stopped jerking on the chain and stood staring at me. I intended to release him. Joe, standing next to me, reached out saying, "No," then listed all the logical reasons why it was wrong to interfere: it would be stealing, I might get bitten, what the repercussions could be from the trapper. Regardless, I wanted to free that coyote.

Finally, Joe persuaded me he was right. We returned to our vehicle, with the understanding that he'd return to put the coyote out of its misery. We drove home in silence. I ran into the house, told the boys their father needed them.

After they left, I sat down and cried. Wiley would no longer be checking out Janny's rabbits or our poultry.

HATCHER PASS

One day an urge to spend a day away from home, be in peaceful surroundings where the life blood of the land flows from the mountains, eat a meal I hadn't cooked, and leave a table covered with dirty dishes for someone else to clean up, motivated me to the rustic, Motherlode Lodge on Hatcher Pass Road. A friendly waitress wandered over, refilled my coffee mug and asked if I planned to pan for gold in the creek across the road. "Not today," I told her.

As she walked away, memories flooded my mind of the hours spent squatting on a bank, swirling icy water over a gold pan partially filled with gravel and sand scooped from a creek bed, hoping to find what someone else missed.

No matter the size of a nugget or flake I gleaned, my heart always beat faster, my lungs pumped harder to push out excited shallow breaths, and my mind ignored my cold hands. At those moments, it was easy to understand what drove miners to suffer hardships in their search for gold.

Sipping my after-lunch coffee, I thought about the drive there. Fourteen miles farther back, just before the pavement ends, the road crossed the Little Susitna River. Tumbled boulders smoothed and rounded by decades of raging, crystal clear water pounding over them had finally settled in the riverbed. I stopped to watch colorful rainbows captured in spray shooting into the air. While I stood lost in the beauty, Missy, my dog, who accompanies me most of the time, explored the banks confining the turquoise water. Nose to the ground, she scrambled through willows, aspen, grass, moss, and daisies to sniff out many unseen messages left by other animals that had visited the area.

An hour later, we climbed back into the car and drove beside the river for a few miles before the road rose steeply and started its climb from the valley floor. At a roadside pond we saw beavers. Busy repairing their dam wall where a moose had punched holes while crossing to the other side, they paid us no heed but knew we were there. Our next stop; one of the many turnouts which overlook switchbacks on the road below, grass covered foothill, craggy peaks in the background, and wild flowers. Threading its way across the valley floor, the Little Susitna meandered through the countryside.

Missy, chasing a myriad of ground squirrels living in tunnel infested ground, disappeared into the brush. While she occupied herself, I had time to scan the surrounding hillsides for bear and moose. Over the years I spotted four bears trundling along the mountainside, all at a safe distance. I also spied a hoary marmot peeking out from a pile of rocks. Thirsty, Missy returned thirty minutes later, tongue hanging out. She willingly jumped into the car, and instantly fell asleep until I parked in front of the lodge.

After lunch, before driving away from the lodge, I offered Missy the few pieces of hamburger and a handful of fries I had saved for her. Both now refreshed, we hiked one of the many trails.

We tramped amid a carpet of berry shrubs. We'd previously visited that spot to harvest the crop of wild fruit in early fall the previous year. I marveled at the patchwork of colors: fuchsia Fireweed, tan grasses, rust colored leaves, red, salmon-pink, and blue berries under a late summer sky.

At the top of the ridge, where I always had an urge to belt out, "The hills are alive with the sound of music," (but refrained from doing so because my voice sounds like rusty hinges,) Missy and I sat side by side. She sniffed the air, deciphered its messages and instantly knew more of our surroundings than me. Three hours later; back at the car I poured her another drink.

I have no idea how many times I've roamed those hills over the years of living in Alaska, but I do know it is a place where my heart, mind, and soul are at peace. It is true wilderness: alive, always changing, exciting, interesting, and untamed.

We drove four miles farther along the road then

turned off onto Gold Cord Road, a road that gives year round access to Hatcher Pass Lodge and Independence Mine. I parked, left Missy to catch a nap then strolled up to the door of the A frame structure. On the way I noticed small cabins dotting the grounds, and a sauna down by the creek. I had never kept a promise to myself to spend a night there. Inside the lodge, from the large restaurant windows, I enjoyed the view of hills and dales.

I remembered a winter day spent with my cold hands wrapped around a cup of hot chocolate while sitting at the same table. I had watched snowmachines slicing new trails through virgin snow sparkling in the afternoon sunshine. Skiers, bundled up and goggled, rooster tails flying out behind them, sped down the slopes. Children struggling to drag sleds up hill passed others who looked like laughing, giggling snowballs rolling toward their smiling parents patiently waiting at its base.

As I left the lodge, I peeked in the car to check on Missy. She was asleep. I walked the short distance into the 271-acre park where Hatcher Pass Park's Visitors Information Center stands. I entered the old building and learned that 30,000 visitors passed through there in 1999.

Pamphlets concerning guided tours through the old, bunkhouse, mess hall and warehouse lay on a table. I stuffed one in my pocket. Before leaving, I studied pictures hanging on the walls of mine activities in years gone by, then walked outside, snapped photos of seventy-some year old machinery used prior to the time the mine closed.

Later, homeward bound, head filled with tales of yore, imagination free to run, I stopped at a pullout where Missy and I climbed from the car and sat on a rock to watch the late night summer sunset paint the sky. Overhead, a lone raven winged his way to a nighttime roost. Picking up color from the sky streaked with gunmetal gray and blood red, the snowcapped Talkeetna Mountains beyond the 3,886-foot Hatcher Pass, flushed pink.

The muffled sounds of men, pickaxes striking granite, and creaking wagon wheels seemed to fill the silence.

Looking across the valley I noticed a wispy, wraithlike image floating along a distance hill. Was it the ghost of Robert Lee Hatcher hoping to stumble across another three-foot ledge of quartz veined with gold as he had in 1906? A light breeze caressing the hillside re-arranged the misty shape, then as light faded and night pushed day aside, it dissipated.

Back inside the car, Missy beside me, I glanced at the clock on the dash. We had been in the hills for ten hours. She'd had a good day; we both had. Time to return home.

BLEM SCOTER
AND THE
TERRIBLE TWOSOME

The Sand Hill Cranes gathered for their migratory flight south. We watched them fly over while listening to their musical voices. Most ducks, swans, and geese had already flown to an area where open water, warmer weather, and food were plentiful. However, there were a few stragglers.

Blem Scoter was one of them. At the time he arrived at our house, he should have been thousands of miles south of Interior Alaska, but a broken leg had prevented it.

For approximately twenty years we had held all the necessary permits to aid injured, sick or orphaned wildlife. Delivered to us by a member of the Alaska Fish and Game Department, Blem Scoter arrived in a cardboard box.

I opened the box to see the poor little injured bird. Injured, yes. Poor little, no. That critter was the most ferocious duck in the world. If he'd had fangs instead of a beak my hand would have been shredded.

Avoiding his attacks, I managed to get one hand behind his head, the other I placed under his soft, down and feathered body in order to remove him from the box.

An attractive duck, black wings except for several white feathers close to his body, a white-eye patch, and a black, white and reddish orange beak. I guessed he weighed approximately two pounds.

Once out, Blem grabbed my sweater along with a piece of skin. Shaking his head as hard and fast as he was able, he pinched until he raised a blood blister on my stomach. Joe covered his head, which calmed Blem down, and he then released his hold.

Upon examination of his leg, I found the bone protruding through the skin. After splinting it with a small syringe split in half lengthwise, I placed him on the floor. Beside a houseful of people, various four legged inhabitants, and the splint on his leg, he had a lot of adjusting to do. Within a week he grew accustomed to us, was far less ferocious, and allowed us to scratch him under his chin.

One of the four legged inhabitants was a premature baby lamb we called Sally, another, a premature kid goat named Sugar Foot. They spent a lot of time inside the house. Both bottle-fed since birth, they were great friends, spoiled, and possessive of me, their surrogate mother. If they were outside and the back door was opened, they made a mad dash for the house, then across the living room to a rug in front of the fireplace, where they promptly parked themselves. How they seemed to love that warmth.

They each had a sack of feed in the kitchen but it seemed they always wanted the other's food. This led to a dance over the sacks, through the dog food dish and water bowl, around table legs, over chairs. Invariably, they managed to trip over Blem Scoter. He hissed at them as loud as his duck-voice allowed.

When we expected them in the house, Blem Scoter stayed in the safety of his box. Those two imps, however, needed to satisfy their curiosity about what the box contained. By the time they finally pushed the lid open enough to see what was in there, Blem seemed anything but impressed with them. He snapped at them, pulling Sugar Foot's ear or the tip of Sally's nose, and hissed. Blem's attack shocked them but did nothing to squelch their enthusiasm. One day Sugar Foot jumped inside the box with Blem, then Sally pushed box and contents around with her black, wooly head.

Blem had a tub in which we arranged a platform so he was able to get out of the water when he wanted, but not out of the tub. Being a Scoter, he was used diving for crustaceans. Because the ponds were frozen and the ground around them covered with deep snow, snails were not something we could supply. However, we could supply him with two filleted Grayling caught during summer to keep his appetite satisfied. The cut up fish sank to the bottom and he dived to retrieve them. When he heard me walking toward his tub, he paddled over toward the door, hoping for food.

Originally discovered by a member of the B.L.M., which sounds like Blem when the letters run together, is how we named him.

Sugar Foot, the baby goat, was named for a another reason. The brown bread she loved was usually in the middle of the table. To obtain it involved antics hard to believe. She stood on her hind legs, jumped on a chair and from there to the table. One day she landed with both front feet in the sugar bowl.

Sally, like all lambs, liked to jump in the air with all four feet off the ground. She enjoyed running, skipping, and generally acting like the proverbial spring lamb that gambols in among the daisies. She wouldn't have looked out of place, except for snow on the ground puffing up in little clouds as she went on her carefree way. Wooly, cuddly and cute, made it difficult to scold her for anything she did.

In spring, when the ice in the pond thawed, we moved Blem Scoter outside. As I walked out of the house calling his name, food dish in hand, he left the pond to waddle toward me. When we told our local Fish and Wildlife Officer, he found it hard to believe a wild duck would come when called. He wanted to see for himself. Knowing oysters were Blem's favorite, I walked out with some in a pan, calling, "Blem. 'mere, Blem." Blem promptly ambled up to his dish. We all stood there laughing, enjoying the moment. Mike said, "That's one for the books."

Once winter rolled into our valley again, Blem returned to the tub. He had made no attempt to migrate south to spend his winter at sea. An acceptance for his way of life with us seemed to have developed.

Then one day, after returning from a hunting trip, we found Blem Scoter dead. He'd climbed onto the platform in his tub, sat down, put his head under his wing and left us. I like to think his little duck spirit found its way to salty waters, plenty of shell food, and a flock of his own kind.

KODIAK

Like many people who live in Alaska, I have read stories of heroic deeds by dogs. How they dragged drowning owners for icy waters. Saved their own young from burning buildings. Ran more than a thousand miles over snow-covered ground and frozen rivers to deliver serum crucial to villagers dying of diphtheria. How certain ones act in a manner that alerts parents of their child's on-coming epileptic attacks. My Kodiak did none of those things, but he lives in that place inside me where special memories reside.

Joe brought him home to me as a small, ball of gray fluff wrapped in a blanket. Kodiak loved my family, including the cat but bonded with me, shadowing my every move. As he grew, his ancestry manifested itself in a springy gait, long legs, large feet, and black tipped tail. His blue eyes belied his otherwise wolfish appearance. Living in a semi-remote area with no close neighbors we had no concerns for his safety. We should have.

Three months after his arrival, Kodiak was running along a mile of logging trail when somebody shot him from a small plane. We assumed the individual thought they had a wolf in their sights.

I found the entry wound after Kodiak crawled home and immediately called our veterinarian in Fairbanks. Fearing Kodiak would not be coming home, I told our children, "I'll be back soon." With Kodiak lying prone on the seat beside me, the twenty-five-mile trip to town seemed endless.

Finally at the clinic, I lifted him from the truck and carried him into the office to be examined. No exit wound was found, and X-rays failed to show where the bullet was lodged. The veterinarian told me, "Take him home. There's nothing more I can do."

I knew Kodiak's chances were slim. For days he showed no interest in food or his surroundings. We emptied syringes filled with water into his mouth and tried to tempt him with tidbits. Then, the fifth day his appetite returned, and within 6 weeks he was back to his boisterous self.

From then on, having come close to losing him, regardless

of the season, Kodiak and I wandered down to our slough at night after the children fell asleep. We loved our nighttime jaunts. I envied his ability to decipher hidden messages, information unavailable to me because I only knew what I saw and heard. He chased shadows, picked up sticks and tossed them into the night, rolled in the dirt, and swam in creeks. He was a free spirit.

While he amused himself, I re-energized myself from my surroundings. I loved the old logging trail that twisted and turned its way to the slough, where banks sloped gently down to water peacefully meandering through the surrounding countryside. Tall spruce stood along the bank. Shadowed patches of earth beneath them were carpeted with dried leaves and brown needles in early fall and winter; places for wildlife to hide.

Kodiak raced along trails bordered with pale trunked aspens, crossed sparkling creeks, disappeared from view, then returned to me. I often wondered if he came back to check to see if I was all right.

In fall, he chased leaves that twisted and turned in the same wind that forced them from their branches. One evening we heard a muffled sound of prey in distress. Alert at once, Kodiak turned his head, ears cupped to listen once more. Again that sound. He leapt away and followed a well-used moose trail, searching for the source.

I followed him. Like poetry in motion, he snaked through trees along creek banks, past a small pond by an old deserted logging mill. The trail ended in a swampy clearing. There, half-hidden in the marshy ground was the mallard we had heard. Wounded by a hunter, it sat earthbound with a shattered wing. Placing each paw on the ground with extreme care, Kodiak soundlessly moved forward. Then, the final killing rush.

When winter arrived and snow weighted down boughs and covered the ground, my loved escort plowed through the deep crystalline white. His breath launched misty clouds into the freezing air. Nose in the air, he checked messages left by others venturing out.

Breaking my reverie, he bounded back to me and sprawled on the ground, sides heaving. I looked down at him and thought of how much more aware of nature I was in his presence. Following him around, I now noticed where wildlife traveled; trench-like trails of triangular prints left by ptarmigan, otter slides, tiny vole impressions left as they scampered from one place to another, twin-print patterns of ermine that scurried after them.

Over the years Kodiak lived with us, I studied him. I knew his instincts drove him, that he felt joy, affection, loyalty, hunger, pain, and a need to protect us, his family.

There were other things about Kodiak I believe, though I found nothing in writing to back up my theories. I felt sure he was aware of his size and shape. How else could he race through underbrush unscathed or clear fallen trees without tripping? I also believe he knew the extent of his capabilities. However, I do not think he understood that some day he'd grow old and die.

I do know he had feelings of sadness, guilt and pleasure; they showed in his actions. He hung his head and flattened his ears when I told him he must "stay". He acted the same way if I scolded him. His eyes sparkled while he pranced at the prospects of keeping me company on treks through the woods.

In wintertime I watched him hunt white Snowshoe hares. Their shiny black eyes and black trimmed ears gave them away. Sensing danger, the hare crouched lower as Kodiak eased closer. Then panicked, it exploded away. Kodiak lost more than he caught. Sometimes feeling playful and reveling in the snow, he jumped in the air or sprawled on his side to propel along with his front feet and tunnel a trench with his nose. To me, those actions showed expressions of his feelings.

One July afternoon, Kodiak and I climbed 3,000 feet up a mountain. Finding a flat spot, we sat and rested. I poured us a drink of water from the jug I carried. We looked down on the valley at lifeless, skeletal trees left by fire that ravaged the area ten years previously. To an outsider the burn area looked barren but it was, in fact, a mosaic of hiding places for wildlife.

Moose browsed on young willows that sprung up after the fire. Mink, otter and muskrat swam in the lakes. Fox and coyote lived on grouse that nested there. Hawks, eagles and owls hunted there. Dall sheep wandered down from the mountains to drink from the river and eat the first green shoots of the year.

Suddenly, Kodiak swung his head away from me. I turned to look at what grabbed his attention and zeroed in on a grizzly sow with twin cubs. The mother, golden in the sunshine, satisfied her appetite with berries while her cubs played. They tumbled over each other until their mother called them to her side. Soon they wandered off then a coyote trotted out of the underbrush. Kodiak barked but made no attempt to charge down the mountain after it. Instead, he stood, ears erect, nose testing the wind, eyes focused, watching until it disappeared behind a small rise.

In the spring and summer, Joe, my husband, and I often took daytime strolls. One spring day, as we rested on a stump, Kodiak, always attentive, suddenly jumped up and raced out of sight. We heard his barking in the distance.

"Sounds like he's at the house. Let's go see," Joe said as we got up to leave.

Entering the clearing where our house stood, angry, frenzied barking greeted us. We saw Kodiak standing on his hind legs, face pointed up, hackles raised, growling a warning at a bear standing on the roof looking down at him. Momentarily paralyzed I stopped.

Seconds later, Joe pulled me by my arm and we made a mad dash for the door, grabbed a resisting Kodiak by the scruff of his neck and forced him inside with us. Realizing it was only a matter of time before the bear came down, all we could hope for was that he'd leave without smashing through the door.

The Black bear padded over our roof, then a thud told us he jumped to the ground. We waited. The bear grumbled low in his throat, snuffled, scratched at the walls, then sniffed around the door. Kodiak barked incessantly. Joe, 44 pistol in hand, crept to the window with me right behind him.

Ten minutes passed. While the bear sat on his haunches looking at the house, Kodiak kept up relentless barking and howling. The bear stood, lumbered his way to the window, stood and looked in. Now we were eye to eye. After what felt like a moment frozen in time, he ambled off into nearby woods. Kodiak quieted, Joe put the gun away, and I, with the threat of the bear's presence still hammering in my ears, made us a much-needed cup of coffee.

Twelve companionable years passed for Kodiak and me. Then one morning I noticed he didn't follow me to the bathroom, as was his custom. I sensed something was wrong, but couldn't figure it out until two nights later when his whine awakened me. I jumped out of bed to check him. He didn't get up from the rug beside my bed, just looked into my eyes. Unable to read the message he was sending, I sprawled on the floor beside him. He placed his paw on my open palm. Then I knew. His pads felt cold to my touch; his circulation was slowing down.

I called Phil Meyers, our local veterinarian in Wasilla, as soon as his office opened. "Bring him in," he said.

After examining him, Phil suggested, "Leave him here."

I wanted to take him home but agreed he should stay in Phil's capable hands. That evening I took Kodiak a bone. He whined and wagged his tail, but didn't get up to greet me or take the gift I offered. I looked questioningly at Phil, who shook his head.

Before answering the phone early the next morning I knew Kodiak had died. I'd woken with the knowledge during the night. Phil asked permission to do an autopsy. I agreed. After all, the body was now only the husk that had housed the spirit I so loved. "Please call me with what you find," I said before hanging up.

The result amazed us all. The bullet, which was not found twelve years earlier, had been lodged in his heart all that time, finally shutting down his system.

"He should have died when it happened. It's a miracle he lived," Phil told me.

Kodiak had given me unconditional love, and it took me a long time to recover from his death. Memories flooded my mind of days when we were younger, racing through the trees, scattering autumn leaves in our wake. Of companionable winter evenings spent in front of the fire after the family was in bed. Times when he trusted me to take care of wounds, or pull porcupine quills from his face and feet.

For many days I walked around with red and swollen eyes. His image haunted me. I found myself high-stepping over his sleeping place or listening for his footfalls. Each shadow seemed to be of his outline. Everywhere there were constant reminders. Going in or out the house I found myself holding the door open long enough for him to follow, then tried to choke back tears at the realization he never would again.

OUR FIRST WILD PATIENT

As a child growing up in England, I dreamed of Alaska and its wildlife. Raised on a farm, animals were an everyday part of my life. My parents understood my obsession to care for all orphaned, abandoned, or hurt piglets, calves, puppies, kittens, and poultry. They always encouraged my enthusiasm.

Then later, as a young workingwoman, I gathered knowledge available from veterinarians at different clinics where I worked. I spent my evenings reading all the books I could find on how to nurse fur, fin, and feathered creatures back to health. Later, as a married woman, the mother of three children, and living five thousand miles from England it was still my dream to treat and care for wildlife.

After many years in Alaska, we bought forty acres several miles from Fairbanks, Alaska. A year after our move we applied for, and received, the necessary permits from Federal and State agencies allowing us to aid sick, abandoned or injured wildlife. Upon the paperwork's arrival, I thought there was nothing else in life I could possibly want. I had it all; a wonderful husband, three magnificent children, a life in the country surrounded by wildlife, and the opportunity to help wildlings in need.

At times, our home seemed like a Game Park with a variety of wildlings waiting to be returned to their natural life once healed. In my mind it was even better than living in Kenya National Park, married to the Game Warden, which had been my other growing-up fantasy.

Our first patient, a Hawk owl, arrived unannounced under his own uncoordinated efforts. I watched him erratically flap his way through a late Alaskan sunrise, land unceremoniously in the snow close to the house, and knock himself unconscious.

Orlando Stubbs, as we named him, was sixteen inches high, had short legs, gray, black and white feathers, big round eyes, and a broken wing. I cupped my hands around him and carried him to the house.

We were amazed at his gentleness when he regained consciousness and again after splinting his wing when I offered him moose liver. He accepted it from my hand. After he'd eaten, I placed him in a cage. He closed his eyes and napped. To us he looked like a stuffed toy; billowy feathers fluffed out around his body made his appearance almost rotund. Looking at his sleeping innocence, it was hard for me to imagine his predatory beak and strong black talons tearing at prey.

On his second day in our house, Orlando pushed open his cage door and walked onto the arm of our couch. From then on he remained free to wander. The domestic birds and animal inhabitants erupted into panic when he emerged. Some ran for cover, some scurried under beds and chairs, while others simply crouched, hoping not to be seen, it seemed.

Once Orlando hopped to the floor, he was apparently less of a threat. Rajjet, our daughter's Chocolate Dutch rabbit, was the first to investigate the newcomer. He bunny-hopped up to the owl, sat on his haunches, leaned forward, twitched his nose then backed away. Snoots, a hen pheasant with a deformed leg, limped up to Orlando and pecked him between the eyes. It shocked the little owl and caused him to lose his balance. He fell over backwards, landing with feet in the air.

Puff, our daughter's poodle, sauntered up to the little bird for a good sniff, but by that time Orlando had had enough. He leaned forward and pecked the dog on the nose. Making no effort to retaliate, Puff sauntered away leaving Orlando standing on his stubby legs trying to regain some form of dignity.

Orlando sat for hours observing the goings on around him. He bobbed his head up and down, turned it sideways, stretched his neck, which sometimes seemed elastic, and listened with his concealed ears. His eyes didn't move, yet he missed nothing. He swiveled his head around and, at a glance, it was difficult to tell if he faced us or was turned away.

In the wild he supplemented his diet with various foods, but for us, keeping Orlando supplied with a mouse each day was a challenge. Due to the amount of mice he consumed, we figured it would require 1,000 mice to feed him if he stayed in our care for a year. Our children set mousetraps in all the obvious places; feed shed, outbuildings, among hay and straw bales, and in our storage shed. Finally, they had to expand their area; even considered paying their friends to trap.

Trapping mice – actually red voles – had its perils. One day our younger son found a vole caught by its back leg and still very much alive. He retrieved it then raced to the house with it clutched in his hands, charged in and asked, "Please try to help him, Mom. He's hurt." After handing it to me, I carefully placed the tiny broken leg in a pheasant quill. Now we had another patient, a trap line casualty recuperating in a small cage on our bookcase, and one less trapper in the family.

The day we slaughtered chickens for our freezer, Orlando decided to help himself. The boys and I plucked the birds; Joe cut them up on a table set outside, and our daughter packaged them. Orlando hopped up to where Joe worked and picked out what he fancied from the discarded pieces lying in a heap. It fascinated us to watch him eat. He picked up his food with his talons, bent his head and whistled to it several times before grasping it with his beak.

It didn't take long for him to figure out I was his main source of sustenance. He came to me often when hunger struck. I placed a vole on my lap. He hopped onto my knees, grasped the mouse with one foot, picked it up with his beak, tossed his head back and swallowed it, whole.

He appeared to enjoy being stroked at the times we placed our fingers on both sides of his body, gently stroking his face. He closed his eyes and relaxed to the point of toppling over if we removed our hands away too quickly. When we lifted one stubby leg to place his foot on our finger then did the same with the other foot, he allowed us to carry him.

Orlando spent hours looking out the window, and I often wondered if he thought of his former life and craved to return. There were times I pitied him because of his captive state, but knew when his wing healed he'd be free again. In the evenings when the house was quiet, Orlando and I spent time together sitting on our respective stools in front of the fire. Those were the times I realized that as well as an empty place by the fire he'd leave a gap in our lives when time came to release him.

For me, the hardest part of rehabilitation was giving up the closeness I developed with wildlings. I always had to remind myself their release was what we worked toward.

CATACLYSM

After Thanksgiving, Joe, my husband, entered the hospital once again. When he returned home, we made short visits to town so I could shop for Christmas. Our children's gifts must be mailed early if they were to arrive in time.

I was thrilled when Mark, our eldest son, called from Alaska to say he'd spend the holidays with us. Enthused, Joe and I decorated our tree. I baked pies, and cookies that Mark especially liked.

The evening before Mark's arrival, Joe said we needed to talk. His seriousness frightened me.

"Honey, you know how much I love you, but we need to make a deal. I'll spend this Christmas with you, then you have to let me go."

My heart raced. My head throbbed. What was he saying? I looked at him in utter shock and disbelief. Surely he didn't mean what he said. The look in his eyes told me he did. He'd been ill for several years and was worn out from the continuous struggle and the pain that came with daily living.

Joe died two days after that Christmas. My world crumbled; my life became colorless, barren, and empty. I was floating in an ocean of hurt. How could I go on without him? He was the one who had taught me the meaning of love; the importance of saying, "I love you." I was lost.

A week later Mark had to return to Alaska.

A few years after that, I returned to a place outside Fairbanks where Joe and I had spent many, many hours. Memories saturated my mind as I stood among tall spruce in a grove not far from our old home. As I looked around, recognition set in. Oh, I know that old stump, I thought.

Then, a quick flash of memory of you and I hunting together. Me doing the bird-dogging, searching through the brush and trees for a moose. "There!" I call to you. Then, "No! Don't shoot!" It was that same old wild stump, another year older, still causing an instant surge of adrenalin, like last year and the years before. Remember how we laughed!

There is a difference now, though. You are no longer here with me. This is not a hunting trip for the family meat. This is a return to a place we called home, a venture to find me and remember us.

So, here I am once again, on the same island, looking at the same wild stump. Strange how nothing has changed. It is as I remember. Only I have changed. The peace, quiet, and beauty are as they were.

The wolf tracks are there. Maybe not the same wolves, maybe different beavers in the pond, maybe the same family of squirrels making piles of empty pine cone petals. It is all so familiar. But this time I am a visitor, though not a stranger. This time I will observe differently, see through eyes that look into the past, not the present. That will change I know. I will come to the present and, hopefully glimpse a course for the future.

When you became ill and went to the hospital, the doctor told me you would not be coming home. He said I should tell you anything I wanted you to know. So many thoughts: "Don't leave me. Stay. So many plans. Forty-four is too young to die. I can't do it alone. What about the children? God, don't take him. Why us?"

Selfish thoughts every one of them.

Pulling myself together, I returned to your room. Trying to smile to cover my breaking heart and destroyed world, I sat holding your hand. We talked as you drifted in and out of consciousness. You asked me to go home and get some rest. I didn't want to leave. You didn't want me to stay. Our last hug. One more chance to tell you how much I love you. One last time to hear you whisper, "I love you also."

In the years you have been gone I found I have capabilities I was not aware of. You always had faith in me, but I always looked to you for strength and advice. For so long I wandered, roamed from room to room, inside to outside, and back. Such a lost being. I didn't know what I was looking for, but it must have been your companionship, your influence. You.

We shared everything: love, children, time, sickness, health, money and lack of money, play, gladness, and sadness. We shared our innermost thoughts, our hopes, dreams, fears, and our desires. We knew each other as well as two people sharing a life are able to do.

This island and I have a lot in common. We have both gained new growth. People have come and gone in our lives. Some, leaving tracks that will remain forever; Some, taking parts and pieces; Some, leaving treasures and some, debris.

That old, wild stump and I have a commonality, too. The basic structure has not changed. It stands alone quite strong against the forces that be, yet still there to be leaned upon for support if needed.

Somehow, even in your absence you give me strength. Because of you and your belief in me I am able to face each day doing what is necessary. I try to stand tall in a manner I feel you would approve. Oh, I still have my fears, lots of old annoying habits, ghosts of years gone by, and no real plans for the future. But, for whatever reason, I feel peaceful on this island by this old, wild stump. And tomorrow is another day.

Wherever you are, "I love you."

Joe had been my life, my friend. Our love; all things meaningful: the music of water murmuring its way over rocks, rustling leaves, bird song, sunrise and sunset. The language of one heart to another, more clear than words.

After I returned home, I still had no real goals. One day drifted into the next. I did what I needed to do and life went on. Creeks and rivers still flowed to the sea, and mountains remained solid guarding the valleys below.

Then, one spring eight years after Joe died, Mark made a special trip to Oregon to talk to me. He was concerned about my life and insisted I take a look at the way I lived. I thought I was doing a pretty good job. I took care of my birds and animals, managed my business, kept up the house and yard, and paid my bills.

But he told me, "You need focus, Mom. You need

structure. Think about going back to school."

I argued that at fifty-eight I was too old, but ended up attending a Creative Writing course at the local college the following fall. It proved to be the best thing for me.

How wise our children grow to be!

THE DUMP AND OTHER FUN PLACES

Not a pretty place in summer, the dump is transformed to a place of beauty in winter. The first snowfall covers the ground, turns mounds of garbage into white rolling hills. Quiet prevails, and trees dressed in winter finery, and rose-colored mountains reflecting an early afternoon sunset guard the dump's perimeter. Ravens standing chest deep in the new powder poke their thick, powerful beak into a hidden scrap beneath the snow. Foxes, the color of autumn tinted maples, scrounge for snacks. Eagles perch on naked branches, surveying the scene below them. Huge trucks unload their cargo.

On one dump-run while tossing bulging, black garbage bags over the wall into a waiting truck bed parked below, I heard children laughing. Their father, busy emptying the back of his station wagon, insisted they settle down. I looked into their vehicle and saw two small boys and a girl about six years old who had been reprimanded. One boy, a blond, the other a brunette and the towheaded girl reminded me of my own children at that age. How different trips to the dump had been then.

Before climbing back into my van, I looked around. The area appeared to be generally clean and well organized - barrels for oil, a shed for batteries, and numbered areas where vehicles backed up for patrons to heave garbage bags over a low wall. Only seagulls and ravens seemed to be enjoying themselves. The attendant inside the booth, who took my money, handed me a doggy bone for my faithful companion.

On the drive home, I thought back to the times my husband had said, "O.K., who wants to go to the dump?" and our kids had rushed through breakfast, grabbed their jackets, stuck their feet in rubber boots, then crowded each other out the door. Pushing and laughing they raced to our dilapidated, old, rust ridden, red truck they named Old Yella. For them, the dump always proved to be a fun place, and treasure-trove. They spent hours poking through piles, foothill high, of items people discarded. They gathered old bicycle frames, a wooden horse the boys fixed and gave to their sister, frayed furniture for their fort, pennies and nickels down the side of a worn out couch, and other treasures I have long since forgotten.

When they arrived home, the first thing I required of our children was to change their outfits so I could wash out the odors clinging to their clothes. Eager to work on the treasures they'd retrieved, my demands always brought an, "Oh, Mom. Do we have to?"

They loved every minute of the hours spent restoring or tearing apart those things. With little money and a creative imagination they invented useful and worthwhile items, which often meant more to them than anything store-bought.

The day they and their father brought home a decrepit, chipped refrigerator and a fifty-five-gallon drum with a rusted top, I asked, "What in the world are you going to do with those?"

Sparkling eyes looked back and me. "You'll see, Mom. It's a surprise," came the answer as sideways glances passed between them. Conspirators all.

For weeks that old fridge sat out behind the house. Then, one morning their father said, "Come on boys. We've got things to do." Away they went with their sister who did not want to be left out. Through the open windows I heard hammering, banging and giggling. I couldn't imagine what they were up to, but had been firmly told not to come looking. At dinner that night, one of children told me, "No peeking, Mom. We'll be finished tomorrow, then you can see how ingenious we are."

After lights out, I heard the boys whispering to their sister, "Don't you tell Mom what we're doing."

"I won't," she said in a small voice.

When I checked on them an hour later, they had dropped off to sleep.

The following afternoon, they charged into the house.

"Close your eyes, Mom," one of them said then guided me outside. Once we arrived at the designated spot they told me, "You can look now." They had converted the old fridge into a smoker. Proudly they pointed out the pan where the motor used to be and, said, "That's where the wood chips will burn." Then came a long, detailed explanation of how fish could hang on the newly installed heavy-duty wire rods. I was proud of their accomplishment. They were busting with pride. We used that old smoker for years; even smoked a homegrown turkey or two.

Later that same summer, the children, with their father's help, built a ten-foot stand. They hoisted the fifty-five-gallon drum onto it after painting it a shiny black, removing the rusty top, and then installing a showerhead spigot about two inches from the bottom. They draped a dark green tarp around the stand, leaving a flap for us to enter and exit the stall. The boys filled the drum. The sun heated the water. Using that gravity fed shower was a pleasure for our family all summer long.

Another place our kids enjoyed was the local junkyard. While their father searched for parts he needed to fix our vehicles, they climbed into old cars and, with a loud "Vroom, Vroom," away they drove on some invented adventure. It could have been to anywhere: the jungles of South America, the African Serengeti, the Gobi Dessert in Mongolia, or icebound Antarctica. There were no boundaries to their fantasies. The world belonged to them.

While I understand the reason for things the way they are today at the dump, I'm glad our children had those opportunities while growing up. Their creativity came alive, and they gained knowledge working on projects with their father on things they scrounged from the dump.

THE VOICES OF BONANZA CREEK

As we sat on the bank of Bonanza Creek, I asked Joe, my husband, "Can you hear them?"

"What? What am I listening for? What do you hear?" he wanted to know.

Two days before, we had driven from our home outside Tok, Alaska, to Tetlin where we turned onto the Taylor Highway. For us, that road was the shortest route to the Yukon Territory. At Jack Wade Junction, we veered east on the Top of the World Highway to Chicken. Rumor has it that the people who named that settlement couldn't spell Ptarmigan, the Alaska's state bird.

Along the 200-mile drive, we pulled into a parking lot outside the only store between Tetlin and Dawson City. We bought candy bars and orange juice for snacks, topped off our tank at the pump and headed up the road to Boundary where we picnicked on sandwiches, chips, and the potato salad I'd made the night before.

After lunch we continued on the dusty, graveled road to the U.S./Canadian border. Like all travelers into Canada, we stopped and showed the necessary paperwork to let Customs officers know we were legal, and that the children in our truck were, indeed, ours. Papers checked and found in order, we continued on toward the fast-moving Yukon River. We boarded a ferry to cross, then spent the night at a campground on the outskirts of Dawson City.

As I prepared breakfast on our camp stove the next morning, frying bacon and brewing coffee made my mouth water. After we ate, we washed dishes, packed away the remaining food, then left to sightsee the town.

In town we learned that it was named for George Mercer Dawson, and dated back to 1896. The richest gold strike ever found in North America was first discovered there in a stream called Rabbit Creek, later renamed Bonanza Creek. In 1898, with the arrival of hordes of gold-seeking men, and ladies hoping for a husband, and others intending to make their fortunes from the miners, Dawson City was the largest town north of San Francisco. Women offering men favors for money found it offered them many opportunities. Con men and scoundrels cheated their way to wealth. Originally, Dawson City accommodated 30,000 people. The population is now less than two thousand, except during summer when the city is inundated with tourists, but the city still occupies much of the original site.

Tired by late afternoon, we headed back to our camp. Our children rounded up wood, and Joe built a fire. We roasted hotdogs and marshmallows over the glowing embers then sat on tree stumps around our fire to reminisce about our own past gold panning efforts. We talked about the hours spent crouched on banks hoping to find gold, scooping sand and gravel from creek beds into saucerlike pans.

I remembered the first small nugget I found and the rush of adrenalin and excitement that raged through me. From that moment on, throwing caution aside, I ignored the icy water, cold hands, and worked harder. For the first time I understood how gold fever could take hold. Before falling asleep that night I told Joe, "I don't think I could have made the journeys those miners suffered through. You have to admire their tenacity."

"Yes," he answered. "They had to be a hardy bunch."

Over the years, Joe and our children had found flakes and nuggets. We hoarded our finds in baby food jars with our names on the lids. One large nugget Joe made into a ring for me. I treasure it.

The most notorious route for those hardy miners was the Trail of '98. They traveled by boat from Seattle to Skagway, on foot to Dyea, then over the snow and ice-covered 3,739-foot Chilkoot Pass to Lake Bennett; an arduous trip. To this day relics of cook stoves and bed frames remain along the 32-mile trail.

The miners, 20,000 of them, camped at Lake Bennett. Before that, nobody lived along the windswept icy shores. The men set up sawmills, cut local trees, built boats to travel the last leg of their journey. The lake at the head of the Yukon River offered them a downriver route to Dawson City. Once the ice went out in the spring, enormous fleets of scows, dories, and rafts embarked on the trip to the Yukon Territory. Many boats overturned and lives were lost in the cold and dangerous currents.

Another exhausting and difficult route gold seekers used to reach Bonanza Creek was by steamer around Alaska's west coast to Saint Michael, at the mouth of the 2,000-mile long Yukon River. From there, they traveled on sternwheelers to Dawson City. Hoping to race the ice forming upriver, at least three steamers were trapped in the ice for months, leaving miners and townspeople without supplies. Those building houses, hotels and stores had to wait until the ice went out the following spring before they could resume construction, as every nail and board arrived via the river. With all their wealth they could not change that situation.

In 1898, at the height of the gold rush, a narrow gauge railway, the first railroad in Alaska, which has one of the steepest grades in North America, was constructed. It carried essentials and thousands of miners part of the distance to the gold fields.

As we wandered along the boardwalks in Dawson City, music, laughter, and the sound of a tinkling piano emanated from Diamond Tooth Gertie's. The buildings along the main streets maintained the look of the gold rush town: pink doors on purple houses, green frames surrounding blue doors, lace trimmed windows with scantily clad manikins in provocative poses. How easy it was for us to imagine what life must have been like back then: the grizzled miners, crowded bars, mud streets, busy hotels, bordellos, picturesque sternwheelers anchored at the dock, painfully thin horses, brightly lit gambling establishments, and white painted churches.

A pretty young lady dressed as a cancan girl emerged from an old sternwheeler along the waterfront, greeting us with a smile and cheerful, "Good morning." From her, we learned that the first 8,000 men left the Klondike area in August of 1899, to investigate rumors of huge gold finds in Nome, Fairbanks, and other places in Alaska. "To them," she said. "It must have seemed Alaska was riddled with gold and all they had to do was dig for it, or stumble over it by accident." Some, of course, found it, but for others it was a hard life filled with strife, tragedy, and no gold.

We spent that night on the outskirts of Dawson City at a different campground close to Bonanza Creek.

Now, sitting on the bank watching our children skip rocks in the creek, Joe asked me once more, "What am I supposed to be hearing?"

Slightly frustrated that he couldn't hear what I heard, I left my family and walked along the bank away from them. The voices I heard, and a pull I didn't understand, drew me still farther upstream. I stopped at a place where treetops met above me to form an overhead arch. Little sunlight penetrated the dusky interior of the tunnel created by the leafy cover. Beneath them the crystal clear water rippled by.

Louder now in the quiet, I heard the murmur of men hard at work, the clank of gold pans, and the ping of pickaxes striking rock. I turned and looked around but saw nobody. Ghosts, I thought. Why not? This is a place where men invested hearts and souls into their hopes and dreams. Why wouldn't part of their spirits remain?

I'd been drawn to other places. One in particular stands out. That time I remember standing in total terror unable to move until I convinced my frazzled mind I needed to get away. Even my dog refused to set foot on that island. He turned tail and streaked out of sight. For months after that the event infected my dreams like a virus. Several years later, I learned that at that place someone was murdered.

Now, as I stood mesmerized by the ghosts of Bonanza Creek in this ethereal place where the past was captured, a raven's call broke the spell. I returned to my family. Our children were wading in the stream, turning over rocks, and looking for gold. Joe contentedly sat in the same spot where I left him.

"You've been gone a couple of hours. Did you meet

somebody?" he said as I walked up to him.

"No. Why?"

"Oh," he said, "I thought. . ."

"You thought what?"

"I thought I heard voices."

"So did I," I said. "So did I."

DELTA BUFFALO

Whenever I heard the word "Buffalo" it bought to mind, Indians, Buffalo Bill Cody, and the 4,000 animals he slaughtered in a two-year period. The old Wild West, the multitudes of men who slaved at building the railroad that changed the future of America, and Yellowstone National Park. It never made me think of an area around Delta Junction, Alaska. However, that was where I had my closest encounter with the magnificent animals.

It happened one night driving home to Tok after a shopping trip in Fairbanks. Out of nowhere, it seemed, eyes suddenly reflected in our headlights in the road ahead. Our son, Mark, who was driving the Volkswagen Bug we affectionately called Herbie, slammed on the brakes and slid to a white-knuckle halt.

We rolled down all the windows in hopes of seeing what was behind those eyes, and were immediately assaulted by the sound of thundering hooves as a herd of buffalo charged across the highway. Twice the size of our vehicle, their black silhouettes looked gargantuan; more than capable of trampling Herbie. After their disappearance into the night, we sat waiting for our pounding hearts to return to their normal beat before moving on.

When the buffalo appeared, Delta Junction, a small community located at the intersection of the Alaska and Richardson highways, and where the Alaska Highway officially ends, was far behind us. The town itself is situated about half way between Tok and Fairbanks. A few miles from Delta Junction where the pipeline crosses the Tanana River, we passed a sign that proclaimed the spot as an excellent place to photograph the famous oil pipeline.

Delta Junction, named after the nearby Delta River, started out as a construction camp built in 1919. Originally it was named "Buffalo Center," after American bison were transplanted there from Montana in the 1920's.

The fertile land surrounding the town lends itself to agriculture, with approximately 40,000 acres under cultivation. The buffalo wander on to local farmland, causing not only damage and frustration, but monetary loss as well. The farmers, naturally upset, turned to the state for help with the situation.

In 1980, the state allocated 70,000 acres where the animals could roam. The area was named the Delta Bison Range. Keeping buffalo confined in the refuge is a continuing problem. We can attest to that. They can and do cross the road at most inopportune moments.

A month after that trip, we decided we wanted to see those Buffalo in the daylight. After an egg, bacon, and pancake breakfast, we packed a picnic basket, piled into Herbie, and headed out on our adventure. We set off at first light to seek out the largest American land animals. Our first stop was Tok which, so the story goes, was patriotically shortened from the name Tokyo Camp, when the Japanese invaded the Aleutians Islands of Attu and Kiska.

Tok is the main point of entry to Alaska for people traveling by road, and is the only town in Alaska that those travelers must pass through twice. Once when they arrive and again on departure from the state. In 1991 Alaska's governor proclaimed the small town, "Main Street Alaska."

As well as places to stay and eat or gas up and go, excellent gifts shops are located close to Tok town center. Athabascan Natives from the surrounding villages produce many of the items sold in these stores: beadwork, birch baskets, baby carriers, and moccasins made from hide.

Leaving Tok behind us, we drove to Jan Lake, where we picnicked and fished for rainbow trout. Then, on to Tanacross, an interesting little community of colorful houses, and home to the once numerous Tanah Indians.

Dot Lake, where we stopped at the lodge for liquid refreshment and a piece of homemade pie, is the headquarters of the Dot Lake Indian Corporation. The local school was established in 1952, and the small historic chapel in 1949.

Fifteen minutes down the road we reached the outer limit of the Bison Range, which lies on the southwest side of the Alaska Highway. That area provides 3,000 acres of grassland for the buffalo to forage in during fall and winter.

"Keep your eyes open," Joe told the children. "We should see them soon." Of course, there wasn't a buffalo to be seen.

Disappointed, we drove on through Delta Junction to mile 241 on the Richardson highway. At a viewing spot, we scanned the area and managed to find a small, black lump on the horizon. "That must be one," I said. "Grab the binoculars from the car."

Our three children, wanting to be first to find a buffalo, had a push and shove contest. Finally, Joe reached in over their heads and brought out the binoculars. He focused on the lump in the distance. It was a herd of about twenty buffalo standing close together. Two hours later the animals ventured closer, then closer still. "Wow, they're humungous," said one of our youngsters.

The bull that came closest must have weighed approximately a ton. He stood about six feet at the shoulders. Surrounded by long hair, his head appeared to be extra large. He had a hump on his shoulders, dark brown wooly hair covering his forequarters, and narrow, hips covered in shiny, black hair. He lowered his massive shaggy head but made no threats. The cows with him were smaller animals and, like him, also had horns. When the small herd lost interest in us they wandered away.

We jumped back into Herbie then drove to mile 1412 to make a quick stop at the Cherokee Lodge. Having already eaten our picnic, food was not on our list of priorities. The lodge carried a full menu, which included reindeer sausage. On the grounds is the Artic Train, which is something to behold with its over nine feet tall and four feet wide tires. The children played on a tire not attached to the train.

The day had slipped away all too fast, and it was time

to return home. On the drive we saw another herd of buffalo standing beside the road. Not trusting them, Mark pulled over and waited to see what their next move might be. After studying Herbie for a few minutes, the animals turned and ambled off into the woods, which suited us just fine.

RAISING RAVENS

By nature I am not a Peeping Tom, but for several weeks one spring I spied on ravens. I used binoculars and a monocular to watch their carryings on, and stood on the precarious edge of an eighty-foot bluff, leaned out as far as I dared in order to get a closer look at their latest antics.

When I first noticed them, they were displaying breath-taking aerobatics and checking out the neighborhood. The next time I saw them, they were courting, flitting around the area, wantonly flirting with wild abandonment. So blatant were they in their amorous pursuit, they even coupled where I could see them. Then, suddenly things turned serious. Both carrying building materials they needed, they constructed their new home. Loud and angry, the male chased off would-be lovers, and argued with those that tried to interfere. Knowing they mate for life, which can be forty or more years, I decided they must truly be bonded.

Some time later, the male sat on a nearby treetop waiting in anticipation of his family. His mate covered their four eggs with her warm, black-feathered body. He brought food to her several times a day, and stood guard while she took short flights, I assumed, to exercise her wings.

I love and admire ravens. Considered trickster by some, revered by others, they are true characters. All a person has to do is look into their eyes to see the intelligence. They are professional thieves, and they delight in causing trouble. They tease my dog, Missy, by calling to her and threatening to steal one of her many bones scattered around my yard, then fly to a limb just out of her reach, where they taunt her with their varied vocal abilities. It drives her nuts, but she falls for their games each time.

Ravens have a long history. During the plague in England, not being particular about their diet, they fed on corpses of the Black Death, and were blamed for spreading the disease. The big black birds were also labeled the Goddess of Death in battle. Clever and resourceful, they are given credit for placing the sun and light in the sky. According to legend, after a raven tricked an old man into opening a box it stole them and gave them to the world.

Often hungry, they are opportunists in their search for food. They eat on the remains of wolf kills, rummage in dumpsters, steal fish from eagles, hang out at fast-food parking lots, and patiently wait for a hunter to finish butchering after a successful hunt.

Whenever I see ravens they remind my of a spring years ago. We returned home from a trip to Anchorage, and found a Fish and Game truck in our driveway. They had brought us four baby ravens to raise and release. Looking inside the box, all I could see were four gaping mouths. Each open red mouth, framed by a yellow beak, was as broad as the black fuzz covered body behind it.

They were perpetually hungry, noisy and messy. However, those four were the most fun birds I ever had in my care. Nobody taught them, but they all learned to talk in raspy, rusty sounding voices, by imitating my talking parrots that lived in our house.

Those four ravens were unlike any other bird I'd raised in the thirty-some years I'd been an aviculturist. They were the most playful and mischievous. After their release, they stayed around our house causing all manner of mischief. One of their biggest delights was tormenting King, a Greenwing macaw I purchased from a man who had taught him to cuss, and no longer thought it was funny.

When King spent time outside, the ravens sat on either side of him on a fence and played leapfrog or pulled his long, red tail feathers. They crisscrossed over him until, in desperation, he climbed down the fence, swearing all the while, and flew off to a tree as far away from them as possible. Sometimes they followed him. He cussed them again, flew to the house and knocked on the door with his beak, yelling, "In. In," until one of us opened the door.

Once their favorite plaything was safely inside, they flew to the roof and stamped their feet, which sounded like an army in hobnailed boots from inside. Frustrating as they were, we loved them.

Carved into the top of totem poles, ravens are honored by Natives. Believed to be pranksters by nature, those four lived up to their reputation. They raised more havoc than anyone could imagine. While our daughter and I set out seedlings in our garden, they hopped along behind us and pulled them out of the ground then threw them up in the air. They picked the heads off every yellow flower they found, totally destroyed my hanging-basket Begonias, and terrified our turkeys, geese and chickens by dive-bombing them. Then, with sparkling ebony eyes, they sat on the fence and watched the terrified fowl scatter around our yard.

The times they wanted our attention, they sat in a row on the porch rail, loudly squawking. They talked to all the wild birds that would listen, and when a car drove up our driveway they flew to a tree, waited until the occupants climbed out of their vehicle then said, "Hello," in a rusty-hinge voice. People, always surprised to find out it was ravens and not one of our many parrots talking, asked, "Oh, did you split their tongue?" Then I had to explain that is not only a myth, but also it is cruel.

Unlike those four ravens, the wild male atop a tree below my window does not speak. One morning, he managed to sneak off with one of Missy's smaller bones. I watched him settle on the ground, drop it then cover it with dead grass that he pulled up by the roots. When finished with his project, he hopped away and examined his work. Apparently not satisfied, he returned to his treasure, uncovered it, moved it a few paces to the left then recovered it before returning to his watchtower.

Protective of his mate and future family, a part of his daytime duty was to keep troublemakers away from the nest. I saw him chasing hawks and magpies from his territory; heard him daring them to return. As darkness crept across the valley, he moved to a lower branch where night hunters could not immediately spot him. He was close enough to defend his mate should an owl have chosen to land in the tree and quietly ease along a branch toward her.

It wasn't long before his days grew considerably bus-
ier. He not only had to provide food for his mate but for
his three newly hatched, constantly hungry youngsters
as well. I sympathized with him. I'd been there. However, unlike him standing out there guarding their nest
in wind, rain, sleet and snow, I raised baby ravens in the
warm, comfortable surroundings of our home.

SQUEAK

Squeak, a red squirrel that lived with us, was not confined in any way. He just lived in our house, and there were times we wondered if we lived in his house. He was as wild as he felt he needed to be, yet as much of a pet as we required of him. The choice was his. Our relationship perfect.

Three years prior to his moving in with us, we had bought that house in the country, which had been uninhabited for years. It was totally vandalized, with only the outside walls and roof remaining, both in need of repair.

We wandered from room to room rebuilding and redecorating in our minds as we walked through. When we reached what used to be the bathroom, we heard tiny feet scrambling down a log wall and across the floor. We turned just in time to see a squirrel departing through a window opening. After she left, we poked around in the remains of the closet and found her nest. It contained several babies that still had their eyes sealed shut. We left them undisturbed.

We wondered if when we started to work on the house, and it would be filled with the sound of pounding hammers, whining saws, and people noises, if the noise would bother the mother squirrel. We hoped not. We wanted her to stay. Every time we went out to work we took along "goodies" for Missy, as the children named her. She never ate while we were there but everything was always gone when we returned.

Before we moved into our new home, we made Missy a little log cabin from small birch tree branches. We attached it to the outside of our house. It seemed only natural to us that she would move out when we moved in. She did.

The first night we lay in our bed we watching her carry out her family one at a time. Apparently she approved of the housing we provided. She settled herself and her babies into their new home.

About a month later, Missy shooed her babies off to fend for themselves. They stayed close by but she no longer shared food or the cabin with them. They were, it seemed, as far as she was concerned, big enough to be on their own.

When fall arrived, Missy left. We watched her preparing a midden not far from our house. Within a couple of days one of her young ventured back to his old home, the cabin on the outside of the house. He was there regularly. We left food for him, which he stored in our house and the garage. He hid food in every conceivable place: old bicycle tires' hanging on the walls, cans dangling from nails, and up on the rafters. Inside our house he stored pounds of pinecones and mushrooms he had previously set out to dry on spruce branches.

The colder it became outside the more time he spent inside. He was not at all bashful about being seen while on his exploration trips throughout the house.

It was not long before he discovered the dog food dish. That became a continuous source of food for him, but that was by no means the only thing he hauled away. He took bread, cup cakes, cookies, crackers, and most anything we forgot to put away. He even took color crayons. He stored those things in every imaginable place: behind pictures, in pleats of drapes, on bookshelves, in parka hoods, under cushions, in boxes, drawers, and cabinets.

He stole cotton from the ironing board, rags, insulation, yards and yards of toilet paper to make a comfortable, warm, cozy place to sleep. He made his winter bed in the same closet where he was born.

Every morning he called to us from our bedroom closet, and happily chattered until we awoke. If we pretended to be asleep and not acknowledge his calls, he became agitated and his chattering turned to scolding. Once he was satisfied he had our attention, he ran to the flour can on the kitchen counter where we fed him every day. It was not, however, patiently.

We never touched squeak, but if he felt the need for contact he came to us. He came to our bed while we slept and sniffed around the pillows. One day he sat on Joe's forehead while he was sleeping, but as soon as Joe moved, Squeak scampered off leaving tiny red scratches from his claws.

We could usually tell when squeak had been busy during the night or when we were not home. He left footprints in the butter. He seldom ate it but seemed to delight in running through it.

We spent three winters sharing our home with him. He was as much of a joy the day he left as the first day we found him and his mom. In my minds eye, I can see him sitting on his flour can with his little "hands" folded while he watched me. He and I spent many companionable hours together, especially during the long, dark, cold winter months. My inner ear still hears, his, "Qui, Qui," call coming from the bathroom closet.

THE HAWK THAT STOLE MY HEART

Our house already looked like a zoo when Mike, our local Fish and Wildlife Officer, called to say, "Got something for you. I'll bring them out." Besides our three dogs and Tiger, the cat, we had a Snowy owl, a Red fox, two Boreal owls, two Snowshoe hares, a duck, a mink, and a Goshawk all waiting to be released when healed. A lamb and two kid goats were being bottle-fed, and King my Greenwing Macaw, talked to all of them.

We'd been rehabilitating critters for years so when Mike, a Federal Fish and Wildlife Officer, called and said, "Got something for you. I'll bring them out," I didn't question him.

When he arrived, my husband, Joe, and our three children, Mark, Scott, and Janny, peeked in the box he set on the kitchen floor.

"Where'd they come from?" I asked as I looked down at baby Red-Tailed hawks.

"Confiscated them at the border," he replied, referring to the Alaskan/Canadian border, a hundred miles away. The people who had them planned to use them for falconry. Check them out."

Bending over to get a better look "I only see two," I said.

"No, there are three."

I lifted one out and handed him to Joe, who made sure taloned feet couldn't grab him. Fully feathered and about sixteen inches high, but still yellow at the sides of his beak which showed his immaturity, he looked more than half-grown. The second bird, brighter yellow at the mouth and less feathered, I gave to Mark.

Now I could see the third chick. She looked prehistoric with her pink skin punctuated with black dots. With a pathetic peep she scrunched in a corner trying to hide. In that moment, that funny baby bird stole my heart. "It looks like - kind of like a tiny pterodactyl, Mom," Janny said. She couldn't have offered a better description.

Cupping my hands around her body, I picked the baby up, cuddled her for a moment then nestled her in our daughter's arms, saying, "What do you want to call her?'

"How about, Roo? She reminds me of the, Winnie The Pooh story. Remember when Roo said, "After I learn to jump, I'll learn to fly."

"I like that, Sweetheart. One day this baby will jump and fly."

As I walked Mike to his truck, he said, "They're all from the same nest. The eggs laid at different times accounts for their size difference."

"We'll do our best," I told him as he drove away, but wondered if we could save the baby. It was bad enough that poachers had stolen the older birds, but why hadn't they left the smallest chick for the parents? She could easily die.

We brought in a four-by-six-foot cage and set it on the counter, then placed the hawks in among the sticks and chicken feathers our children had gathered. The hawks were too young to perch. "That's pretty close to their nest," I said.

Roo snuggled into the feathers. The eldest stood glaring at us through the cage bars. Mark said, "He looks like he's in prison. Let's call him Joliet after the one in Illinois. Scott named the next youngest Jonathan, after the well-known seagull. He stared off into space ignoring his surroundings and us. His attitude seemed to be, "I can't see you; you can't see me."

Thinking Joliet would be the easiest to feed, I offered him previously cut up pieces of hare, hide and all. He wasn't interested, but with Joe holding him and my forcing small pieces of meat into his mouth then clamping his beak shut, he swallowed. Next came Jonathan. Still too young to be afraid, and ravenous, he picked up and ate the meat presented to him.

Now it was Roo's turn. As the baby, she was only used to regurgitated food from her mother's beak, so the moose liver I placed in her mouth she let fall out. Holding her beak shut didn't help. I gave up until we could come up with a better idea.

"Give me a few minutes," Joe said. He returned with a smile and a clothespin filed to a point. "This should do it," he said.

It did. I covered my hand in a towel, leaving only thumb and forefinger free to hold the pin. Able to hold small pieces above her head at the same angle she'd been fed by her mother prompted Roo to open her mouth. Our first hurdle was overcome. Maybe she wouldn't be so hard to raise. Over the next two weeks, to my great joy Roo blossomed.

About two weeks later, I heard Joe's voice full of surprise. "Honey, come look at this."

There at the back door stood an immature Bald eagle with a broken wing.

"Did the kids put him there?"

"I don't know," Joe said. "I sent them off to get wood. We'll ask them when they get home."

I picked up the eagle saying, "All right, big fella, we'll make room for you," then carried him inside to set his wing. Before the door closed behind me I called out, "We need another cage."

"Be right back," Joe answered. We had cages to fit anything from a chickadee to bear cubs.

Joe came back whistling and asked, "What'll we call him? He looks dignified like my old English teacher."

"How about Oliver? He reminds me of a government official friend of my father's. His name was Sir Oliver."

Seeing Oliver in a cage when they came in after unloading the wood, Scott asked, "Where'd he come from? Did Mike bring him?"

Joe told them he had found Oliver standing outside the back door, then said, "We have no idea how he got there."

"Guess he must have seen the sign in the sky; the one that reads, "Help Available," Mark joked.

Soon Joliet and Jonathan learned to perch, but Roo, now partly feathered, still strutted around in the jumble of sticks and feathers. They'd been with us for five weeks and now it was time for them to go to the greenhouse away from constant human contact. Oliver would remain in the house for a while longer.

One night I heard his talons clicking on the kitchen floor. I jumped out of bed. There he was strutting across the room with yards of bandage trailing him. "Oh great!" I told him. He looked like an unraveling mummy.

He stared at me while I gathered up the yards of bandages, and felt to see if the bones were still aligned. They were. I lifted him onto the table and re-wrapped his wing close to his body so he couldn't move it. As I worked I told him, "Oliver, don't do this again." After placing him back on the floor, I said, "Goodnight," and returned to bed.

Several days later Joe and I put the hawks in the greenhouse, after he and the boys removed the polyethylene cover from three fourths of the forty-foot building and covered that portion with chicken wire. This arrangement kept them safe from other predators: ermine, mink, adult hawks and lynx. Plus, they still had a place out of the weather when they wanted it. We nailed branches at distances that allowed them to run and hop up onto to perch, and gave them a birdbath. They were not impressed.

Days later, clouds rolled into our valley and settled on the mountain ridges. A storm erupted. As thunder rumbled, the hawks ran back and forth until rain came, then they stood in the uncovered portion of their home, wings open to let droplets roll over their head and down their back. Something about the rain must have triggered their desire to bathe because every day after that, they hopped in their birdbath, dunked their head, dipped their chest into the water, and then gave themselves a good shake before folding their wings.

Oliver, Joliet, and Jonathan fed themselves, but Roo was still being handfed, which must stop if she was to survive in the wilds. She must be independent of humans. She went without food for two days following my decision. Tough love. Hungry on the third day, she wasted no time in pouncing on the remains of a hare something else had killed – another hurdle passed.

In the first week of August, it was time for them to fly. I hadn't expected any problems. After all the books on falconry stated, "A falconer simply...." Well, this falconer didn't simply...." I started with Joliet, the eldest. He attacked when I removed the hood meant to calm him. As he lurched for my face I simply dropped the hundred-foot nylon tether attached to the leather jesses wrapped around his leg, and he "simply" flew away. Our boys retrieved him from a tree. Apparently he was ready to go solo. The next day I threw him into the wind, with Joe and the children nearby. Joliet opened his wings, rose into the air, then settled in a tree.

Two days later, I took Oliver from his pen for another of his many therapy sessions. His wing needed strengthening. I stretched his now healed wing to its full extent, held it for a moment while he tried to fold it then I released it so he could.

The following morning it was Jonathan's turn at solo flight. Not as wild, he didn't attack me when I set him on my arm. Instead of flapping his wings, he lost his balance and simply fell flat on his feathery little face a few times. He clung onto my arm a bit too tight for comfort, and seemed relieved when returned to his home. Over the next ten days he progressed to the point of being released to join Joliet. "Two down, two to go," I told Joe.

Now with Oliver's wing fully recovered, it was his turn for special attention. I donned heavy leather gloves. He stood on my arm, jesses attached. "You want your freedom? Prove you can fly. Ready?"

He opened and flapped his six-foot wings. I felt as though I was standing beneath a helicopter blade. And for a speck in time, thought he'd lift me off the ground, but no, flapping was all he wanted to do this time.

I couldn't decide if Roo didn't know she was supposed to fly or if she was simply lazy. Maybe she enjoyed walking! With the sweet feel of summer fading, and clouds whispering of coming snow, she must try. She wasn't designed to survive an Alaskan winter. "Time's slipping away, Roo. You've got to get airborne today. South is calling you, young lady."

She cocked her head sideways, looked at me, then sat. I forced her onto my arm. Once there, she flopped back and forth like a tightrope artist in a high wind while I struggled to keep her from falling. Her head bobbed up and down, and she half-heartedly flapped her wings. She basically mastered the art of balance that afternoon. Nodding with satisfaction, I returned her to her home.

Frustrated over Roo, I told Joe, "Let's concentrate on Oliver." His wing was strong and his spirits good. I took him outside; held high above my head. He flapped his wings harder and faster, finally releasing his hold on my arm. He flew into the trees. Then something went dreadfully wrong. He crashed through the branches, ending up in a heap on the ground. The sound of snapping twigs drove a ramrod of fear through me. I ran to him. "Oh, no," I said picking him up. His wing had snapped again.

I reset it. He didn't resist, which wasn't like him. He was too docile. No question now, he'd stay through the winter. Would Roo also be keeping him company?

With Jonathan and Joliet perching close by in a tree, I hoped they'd be the encouragement Roo needed. Then, one morning a few days later, Jonathan flew over the yard. To add to my enthusiasm Joliet glided over and landed on a post. I brought Roo out. Surely, seeing her nest mates, she'd fly today. I raised my arm. Losing her balance, she tightened her talons. With blood running from my arm, I returned her to the greenhouse.

"Joe, I don't know what to do with her. She must learn to fly."

Lying in bed that night, I pondered if she would be strong enough to evade wild hawks if they attacked her. Could she catch live food?

I put a live chicken in her cage to take care of the live food part, but I hadn't counted on her getting a bone stuck in her throat. Later, I found her lying on her side gasping for breath. "Don't you dare die on me," I told her as I ran to the house with her held tight.

Once she was on the table, Joe forced her beak wide open. I reached in with tweezers. Oliver, not caring if she lived or died, looked on. The jagged bone raked across the inside of her throat. Blood dripped from her mouth. "Oh, Roo," I whispered. She took a shuddering breath, struggled to her feet then latched onto my hand with a talon. Now both of us were bleeding, but at the least, she was alive.

"Mom, why do you do this? Don't you get tired of getting hurt?"

"Mark, I can't give up on them, any more than I would if one of you were hurt. They're family too."

Joe carried Roo out to the greenhouse to finish recovering.

To my surprise, the next morning she was running and flapping back and forth the full length of the greenhouse. I was ecstatic. My timing had been off, not hers. She obviously had the desire to fly. She flew within that week.

Yet now, after fourteen weeks with Roo, I wasn't sure I was ready to let her go. I saw her as much more than just another efficient predator. She'd been the baby, the most helpless, the most dependent, and she'd stolen my heart the day she arrived, but deep down I knew that like all wild creatures designed to ride the wind, she must be free to soar.

We released her on a sunny, mid September day. She raised and lowered her powerful forty-two inch wings as Joe and I watched. The children cheered her on. "Go, Roo, go."

"It's going to feel like this when our children leave home," I whispered to Joe. "Only worse."

"Let's hope they're as well prepared," he said, giving me a quick squeeze.

But, what was to become of Oliver? Would he spend his entire life in the pen we built? I felt as if I'd failed him.

Not long after that, Roo winged in over the house, calling all the way. Our family, including Oliver, watched as she started her climb. Up, up, and up she went, gracefully riding the wind. Soon she was a small dot in the sky, and then she disappeared.

"Talk about the ugly duckling." I said. "She is as elegant as any swan in flight."

That was the last time we saw her until the following spring. It was then that I heard her distinct whistle as she flew toward her old home. Later that year she found a mate and raised young not far from the house. Roo never failed to call as she flew over, but her mate seldom came close.

Postscript

A year later, the Fish and Wildlife Department in Anchorage called. Oliver was needed for a Captive Breeding Program. His life was going to be meaningful after all. Knowing that eagles mate for life, we were excited for him. He soon joined the Springfield Zoo in Missouri.

TRIP TO SOUTHEAST

Getting to Gustavus, Alaska, was easy. Leaving there was another matter, which had nothing to do with the various means of transportation to and from Juneau. Several small airlines have scheduled flights. The Auk Nu Fast Ferry, a catamaran type boat, and Alaska Airlines all carry passengers. No, leaving Gustavus was a heart felt thing that started with the friendliness of the local residents who have a built-in talent that made me feel instantly at home.

The Southeast community of approximately four hundred, the splendid scenery, pristine wilderness of the surrounding countryside, and the wildlife all contributed to making it a place I'll long remember. A black bear shimmied up a Sitka spruce tree a few feet from where we stood watching.

The snow and glacier dotted Chilkat Range and Fairweather Mountains encompass three sides of Gustavus. The fourth is open to grassy flat lands and sand beaches along the Icy Straits. From nearby Bartlett Cove, cruises leave daily during the summer to visit sixteen spectacular glaciers in the area. Guided hiking tours, one to six hours long, are available for those of us who enjoy walking, but if you're a meanderer like me it may take longer.

The flat fertile land and coastal climate of Gustavus appealed to farmers who originally settled there in the early 1900's. Over time, agriculture has given way to tourism.

Gustavus is the gateway to the clear, deep waters of Glacier Bay and the Icy Straits, which are abundant with marine life. Like other tourists we saw Orcas, Humpbacks, Sea otters, dolphins, sea lions, and salmon.

Gustavus is not a thriving metropolis, which was fine with my friend and I. We found exactly what we wanted. Peace and tranquility. The added bonus was the warmth of the people who live there. Drivers and passengers waved to us, and those on foot or a bicycle called out a jovial, "Hello."

Gustavus, which used to be known as Strawberry Point, does not lack for things to do. There's kayaking, bicycling, fishing, whale watching, sightseeing, hiking and golf. Not golfers, my friend and I did not take advantage of the nine-hole course where clubs and handcarts are available for rent. We did, however, ride bicycles provided by the inn. Having not ridden for years, I discovered muscles I had long forgotten existed. It was fun and, I'm sure, hilarious to watch as I wobbled my way down the driveway trying to keep the bike out of the tall grass and trees.

I left Gustavus with mixed emotions. The place and the people had worked their way into that special place in my heart where I hold memories dear. To try to offset my lack of desire to leave, I reminded myself that Skagway, and a new adventure, was waiting for us.

At the airport, quivering like a racehorse at the start gate, the small, single engine plane on the runway, motor running, was ready for takeoff. Small balls of moisture rolled across the cockpit windshield. The pilot, a man no longer young but obviously experienced, melded into the seat behind the controls. His hand, strong and sure, pushed the throttle forward. The five of us, all securely belted in, looked out the window and watched as trees and mountains at the edge of the field turned to an indistinguishable blur. In moments we were airborne, flying toward jagged, snow spotted peaks that disappeared into low hanging clouds.

Slightly apprehensive, I found myself gripping the camera in my hands as the wind buffeted the plane, but soon forgot my nervousness when I noticed herds of goats standing on high ridges as we passed through a narrow valley. What do they find to eat on those barren looking rocks above timberline?

Gustavus, far behind us now, was where we spent time at the Gustavus Inn, which is run by the Lesh family. Originally, in 1928, it was a homestead where husband, wife, and nine children settled to carve out a life from the wilderness. In 1965, the Lesh family converted their home to a country inn. During our short stay, we enjoyed family style dining with fresh cut flowers on each table, and fruit and vegetables from the garden. Fragrant odors of pies, cakes and breads made from scratch emanated from the kitchen. Staying at the inn was as comfortable as being in my own home, with the added benefit of somebody waiting on me.

One day while there we spent three hours on a whale watching tour boat. I'd seen belugas and orcas before, but had not seen humpbacks. However, on this trip they were in abundance. We saw them breach, roll on their side and show us their huge flippers that reached high into the air above the surface. We watched them feed and, standing on the rear deck, totally mesmerized by the magnificent tail flukes displayed before me as a whale prepared to sound, I completely forgot to snap a photograph. Humpbacks, it seemed, were everywhere.

On the trip to where the captain and crew knew whales would be, they stopped long enough for us to enjoy and photograph seals and sea lions. Among the kelp beds we saw sea otter mothers floating on their back, front legs tightly wrapped about fuzzy round-headed babies cradled on their chest. Black and white dall dolphins raced beside the boat and played in the churning wake. For me that trip was the ultimate.

Now, settled in and my apprehension forgotten, the pilot flew us over the small town of Haines. Then, as we followed the coastline, Skagway, with four cruise ships tied at the docks, appeared in front of us. The pilot continued up the valley, turned, then made a flawless landing.

Tired from a full day, we located a motel well away from the hustle and bustle of downtown. After deciding we were hungry, we called for one of the many S M A R T buses, a local source of transportation, to take us to a restaurant for dinner, then back to the motel for an early night. In anticipation of the next day being a full day we piled into bed.

The following morning we soon found that, unlike Gustavus, Skagway is a busy, busy place. Broadway, the main street, is lined with plank boardwalks and old time false-fronted stores, which were crowded with some of the 8,000 vacationers from the cruise ships.

Skagway has a unique history, which started in 1897 with Skookum Jim, Tagish Charlie and George Washington Carmack, and their discovery of gold in the Yukon.

Thousands of men driven by hopes of finding gold poured into Skagway via steamships. Others, along with a few stalwart women, hauled their belongings over miles of the treacherous White Pass and Chilkoot trails. While in White-horse, still others built boats to haul to Bennett Lake and float the equally danger filled Yukon River to Dawson, and then made their way to Skagway, some 600-miles away.

Their journeys were fraught with tribulations: shipwrecks on the Inside Passage, avalanches, and the death of 3,000 malnourished, badly cared for and overworked horses and mules.

As we found out, Skagway survives on tourism. In 1998, 600,000 people arrived by bus, ferry, cruise ships, private vehicles, and planes. When the season was over, Skagway reverted back to its 800-odd permanent residence. During the Gold Rush years the town's population was 20,000.

Our first day in Skagway we decided to ride the green and yellow narrow gauge White Pass and Yukon train in order to travel the rugged mountain terrain up to the 2,865-foot summit. As the engine and refurbished Gold Rush coaches rumbled along the narrow shelf blasted out with 450 tons of dynamite, we learned the history of the stampeders. We passed waterfalls that fell hundreds of feet from their origin high in the mountains, looked down on a raging river that has never successfully been navigated, and saw a 100-ton granite memorial to the workmen who were crushed be-neath it.

A rockslide that occurred after we left town on our ride to the summit closed the tracks. The train was forced to re-turn to Skagway. With our journey cut short, it left us time to walk down Broadway. We encountered horse drawn car-riages operated by folks dressed in 1890's attire, passed a city museum, an abundance of gift shops, and the histori-cal Golden North Hotel with its golden dome. We peeked in the Red Onion Saloon. On side streets we photographed painstakingly restored Victorian houses with immaculate landscaped gardens.

The following afternoon, sitting in a small theater watch-ing the "Days of 98 Show," we learned the history of "Soap-ie" Smith and his motley crew of con men and, the demise of Frank Reid, a surveyor of dubious morals. Jefferson Randolf Smith, or Soapie as he was called, was the ultimate con artist but tried to establish himself as a good citizen. He contributed substantially toward the building of Skagway's first church; aided widows, and founded an "Adopt a Dog" program.

Frank Reid was not impressed by the deeds. After a British Columbia stampeder was robbed of $2,800 in gold dust, Frank and Soapie ended each other's lives in a shootout at the wharf. Frank's bullet pierced Soapie's heart, killing him immediately. Soapie's shot to Frank's groin caused him to die a lingering and painful death several days later. Frank Reid was laid to rest in the small cemetery. Jefferson Randolf Smith, considered unfit to be placed in sacred ground was buried outside its boundaries.

After the show it was time to leave Skagway. We returned to Juneau then boarded a jet back to Anchorage. Sitting on the plane, I thought about this and other trips I'd taken to Southeastern, what a magical place it is, and how I enjoyed the time spent there.

MOSQUITOES

Thousands of mosquitoes swarm around my house, which sits above The Hay Flats, their personal twenty-eight thousand acres breeding ground. They are impossible to ignore in their masses as they hover in clouds around my door waiting for me to step outside to donate blood. I swat at them, missing most, but managing to gleefully eliminate a dozen or more, at the same time thinking, 'Why doesn't the Red Cross hire them?'

Only the females bite but even up close and personal, who can differentiate between the sexes? In my search for some purpose for their existence besides feeding swallows and fish that, maybe, could survive without them, I discovered there are three thousand different species of the nasty little pests. How's that for an unpleasant thought?

While they embed their sucker-straw into my flesh, they enjoy five micro liters of blood each time. Figuring it would take at least a million or more of them to drink me dry, I can only hope the swarms sniffing around me consist of males. With the first stinging puncture my hopes are dashed.

Apparently, I have that special something that attracts them. Simply having warm blood does not necessarily make you an acceptable candidate. I say this because one or two members of my family appear to not produce what mosquitoes are after.

From research on the aggravating little bloodsuckers, I found it all starts with an exhaled breath. Trails of carbon dioxide float away like a ribbon, the mosquitoes zero in on it and then track it to the source. I'm not sure I believe that particular piece of information; I can step outside and not have time to breathe before they start their invasion. Then, having had their way with me, they search out a dark, moist place to lay eggs, thousands upon thousands of them. Contributing to their propagation does not thrill me.

During spring and summer, Deep Woods is my choice of perfume. I never leave home without slathering it on uncovered skin. Somehow though, they never miss an opportunity to zero in on the one or more spots I overlooked. I rub my dog down with the same repellent, which she hates, and they still find a missed place or two around her nose, ears, bare belly, and legs from which to take a swig.

Many of us have heard stories of Alaskan mosquitoes. Some not so true, some true: tales of them carrying off a sled dog team; being designated the state bird; when they fly over they cast shadows as big as helicopters. Those tall tales belong in the 'Yeah right' department. However, on the tundra, caribou have been known to run themselves to death trying to avoid them. Fact is, mosquitoes can suck the life-blood from very young animals.

As far as mosquitoes are concerned, from my point of view, the only reason I find for their existence is the enjoyment of knowing millions of the little beast will meet a violent end.

OUR DAUGHTER'S WEDDING

The first thing on the agenda was a wedding dress. Janny and I went to a boutique in Anchorage. Nervous, I handled myself well until she walked out of a dressing room in a bridal gown. Then I burst into tears. My baby! She was beyond gorgeous. However, in my mind's eye I saw the little girl who had come running to the house looking like a miniature savage, hair and face plastered in mud. Even her clothes were caked. I had swooped her off the ground, intending to hold her away from me, but she wound her arms and legs around me.

Being embraced by Janny at that age was a lot like tangling with an octopus. I carried her to the bathroom and held her up so she could see her reflection in the mirror. Peals of giggles rippled from her as she placed her muddy hands on my cheeks. We then looked like twins. After that she attempted to fluff her mud-packed hair around her mud-smeared face.

Our next project; find a place to hold the wedding. Finally, we all agreed on Settlers Bay, a picturesque building on the edge of a bluff overlooking a valley with a clear view to the mountains; a beautiful setting for their wedding and reception. We arranged food, drink, and seating for family and guests, then off we sped to order invitations and flowers.

The wedding day dawned with a perfect sunrise; a clear sky streaked with orange and pink. Our daughter looked so young and beautiful as she took her father's arm for the last time as Daddy's little girl. I cried while she and Devin exchanged vows then, suddenly it seemed, they were heading out the door to the reception upstairs.

All those dear to us were there: friends of ours who had known Janny since birth, friends of hers through her growing up years, Devin's family and his friends, some of whom we had known since he was fifteen. So quickly, it seemed, the reception was over and, under a shower of rice and confetti, the newly weds sped off to a waiting limousine and a new life together.

A NIGHTMARE

I slipped off to bed early. The fox, whose leg we had amputated, was in our care still and had not killed the chicken, which would prove he could survive in the wilds when released. I suffered through terrifying nightmares of the fox as he made his way toward the hen, an evil look in his eyes, tongue lolling from his open mouth, fangs glistening in the moonlight. His foreleg stretched out in front of him flat on the floor, rump raised in the air as back legs propelled him across the floor. Pools of drool showed in his wake. When the chicken's head lying on the floor, eyes desperately searching for her body, erupted into raucous squawking, and her body exploded into action, blood and feathers flying in all directions, I burst from the dream.

Scrambling out of bed, I raced to the kitchen. Peace reigned. The chicken was still perched on the box. The fox continued to watch her through the bars of his open cage.

I made a hot chocolate to help my jangled nerves. An hour later I returned to bed. The remainder of my night was long and dream filled.

Two nights later the chicken met her demise. We found her remains hidden under a rug in the fox's cage.

GEORGE

Winter silently waited on the other side of the mountains. One day soon it would slip to our valley bringing pristine splendor.

The valley we lived in was located some thirty miles from Tok. Our old log house sat next to Log Cabin Creek, which flowed gently through the property on its way to the Tok River.

When we moved to the area, the population of Tok was approximately eight hundred. Everybody knew everybody else, and if help was needed a neighbor could be counted on to provide it. We had moved there from the Fairbanks area.

Having all the necessary permits issued by the Department of Fish and Wildlife, and the Department of Fish and Game, we had been in the envious position of caring for sick and injured wildlife. Some we had brought with us from Fairbanks, and others we acquired while living there.

"Living out", as the expression goes, we could observe wildlife at its best. The animals and birds dwelt undisturbed, except during hunting seasons.

During spring and summer months we watched the Swallows dive after mosquitoes swarming above the water, saw the Juncos flit from tree to tree. Redpoll Finches with their bright poppy red crowns, and Warblers flew in and out of willow bushes, while Waxwings crowded the treetops. We heard woodpeckers hammering trunks. Sandhill cranes called from on high as they looked for places to land. We watched Marsh Hawks search for prey, and stood in awe as hundreds of Canadian geese flew in their military like V formations on the way to their breeding grounds. Loons, we seldom saw, but heard from a distance.

Hawks were somewhat of a problem to us during the summer months. Goshawks winged down our driveway, gathering speed and swooping into our chicken and turkey pens, snatching a free meal without ever touching the ground.

Although a bird of prey is majestic and has beauty, it was difficult to imagine feelings of any form of attachment developing towards them. They have the appearance of being cold, calculating, and dangerous. Their red orange eyes do not radiate warmth, their hooked predatory beaks do not emit any desire to have one nibble on one's ear, and their talons do not give one the desire to have them land on a bare arm or shoulder. That was probably because they are seldom in a position to be observed in any other light than that of a very efficient predator.

My outlook towards birds of prey changed when George, a large Goshawk, with a forty-six inch wingspan, came to us. He had been caught in a trap set for fox during the winter months, and brought to us by a member of Fish and Wildlife. He was in sad shape. Both feet were frozen, and one leg and wing broken. We splinted his leg, set his wing, wrapped it close to his body then gave him antibiotics. Next, we put him in a sling hanging from inside the top of a cage. He was upright, with no weight on his feet as they barely touched the bottom of the cage. How dejected he seemed. He hung in his sling staring off into space.

The most important thing we needed to do was find him an interest in life; otherwise we'd lose him. I tried to feed him and get him to drink. He refused. A short time later I placed Manfred, my daughters pet mouse, in a such a way that George could see him. When Manfred moved, George instantly was alert. Apparently he wanted Manfred.

Now I knew he was aware of his surroundings I tried to feed him once more. He refused to open his beak. Forcing it open I placed cut up moose liver on his tongue. He closed his beak, and after a few moments swallowed. That seemed to remind him he was hungry. From then on he ate everything we offered.

Daily I removed him from his sling to slather medication on his feet. At night I fed him whole mice, as he needed roughage. In the morning he regurgitated a pellet called a "casting". In the afternoon I took him to the bathtub to soak his frozen feet in lukewarm water.

The sling turned out to be a hazard to his health. He almost hung himself. One morning I found him hanging upside down and unconscious.

The swelling left his feet, but his right foot turned dark, and then an ominous black. A few days later so did his left. Even though his general condition improved, there was no doubt he would lose his feet. His broken leg and wing healed over time. One day, holding him high above my head to let him exercise his wings, I decided to see if he could fly. He flew across the kitchen and landed on the floor. I was so proud of him.

For his efforts I rewarded him with a dead hare. He showed no interest until we poked it with a stick, then, as soon as it wiggled, George pounced on it and "killed" it. He stood on it and tried to hide it by drooping his wings and fluffing out his long body feathers. As he ate, he emitted a high-pitched sound, not unlike that of a radio frequency.

No longer forced to live in his cage, he was free to return to it anytime, which he seldom did. When he walked across the floor his feet, which were completely dried and dead, sounded like he was wearing clogs. He used his wings for support; the same way a person rests on their crutches. He cared for himself by preening his feathers, and trying to pick off his dead feet.

George tolerated Joe and our children, but he could not tolerate strangers. When a stranger arrived he lay on his side, gasped for breath and stared off into space. I told people, "I think he feels that if he can't see you, you can't see him."

We decided he should see our Veterinarian. I worried about the trip, but with George settled in box, off we went. He traveled well. He behaved well, until we met with the Veterinarian. I took George out of his box. He wouldn't stand. He wouldn't fly. He lay on his side gasping for breath. I wondered, how could this man possibly believe all the good things I was saying about this half dead, rumpled looking bird? "The kindest thing we can do for this bird is put down!" he said. Shocked, I stuttered, "You can't be serious! He can fly. He can walk. He can...."

The kindly Veterinarian nodded his head and said, "Uh, Uh. I see."

Bundling up my bird, we left the office. On the trip home

I opened the box. "Oh, George, how could you do this to me?" With the sound of my voice, up popped his head. He hopped out of the box and proceeded to try to fly around the cab of the truck. I put him on my shoulder and that's where he stayed until we reached home. That night he ate ravenously, and slept on the pillow by my head.

When George's feet finally snapped off, my husband made him artificial ones. We attached his new plastic feet to his legs with a neoprene band, and then placed him on the floor. Now he could walk, hop, fly, and land on any flat surface.

We came to the conclusion George and his Creator decided the Veterinarian's judgment had not been right. George had tried so hard to overcome so much, we felt he deserved all the help we could give. He was dependent on us for his very survival, and we would not let him down.

Two short years later, George died. During those years I wondered if he had emotional needs and, if so, what took care of them? Because he had no pain in his feet did that mean he was unaware of his problems and how they affected him? Our house was thirty-two by forty-eight feet, but still a cage to George. What had allowed him, a free flying wildling, to accept his unnatural situation? Because of his attitude it would not have been right to feel pity for him, so I seldom did.

I always felt a strong admiration for him, and will never forget him. He left a profound impression on me, and when I see hawks or other birds of prey, I see them differently because of him. I no longer see only a highly skilled predator.

PADDLES

Once warm weather arrived, our children and I wandered down to a nearby beaver pond. Janny almost tripped over Paddles, a beaver that was hidden by furled-over straw colored grass. He had a fishhook deeply embedded in a badly infected paw. My son stripped off his shirt, soaked it in the creek, handed it to me and I wrapped Paddles in it to carry him home.

To avoid being bitten by his powerful teeth we anesthetized him. Full grown, Paddles weighed about thirty-five pounds. He would have been impossible for us to handle had he been conscious. He apparently had been in a fight and some of his wounds required stitches. Others looked as though they would heal by themselves once cleansed and the maggots removed. His foot required lancing, swabbed with hydrogen peroxide, and sutured.

Once out of the anesthetic, Paddles looked around, checked his new surrounding then drifted back to sleep. The next day, with him tightly held in a towel, I examined his wounds. He remained still until I touched his tender, swollen foot. Then he jerked, hissed, and pulled away from me. With Joe's help I finished working on him. We placed him in a cage. Janny gave him willow branches to gnaw on, and fresh leaves to eat. I packed away our veterinary supplies, while he nibbled.

Three days later the swelling subsided and the redness faded. Joe filled a tub with water and gently placed Paddles into it. Paddles scrubbed his face and combed his fur with his webbed hind foot, which had a double nail on the second toe. His nails look like a beak and he used them in the same way a bird preens its feathers. After he completed his ablutions, I carried him outside to a wire pen near our creek.

He lived with our menagerie for twelve days then we carried him back to the pond where we had found him. He waddled down the bank into the water and swam away without so much as a "Thank you." Bubbles, like a string of jewels, trailed behind him as he vanished into his pri-

vate world and back to his family, leaving me, a landlub-
ber, to imagine how the inside of their home looked.

I had read about beaver lodges and how they are constructed, how the walls are packed with mud to keep out
winter's cold, and body heat in. I stood there wishing I
could follow him to see for myself.

Two weeks later, I walked back to the pond in hopes of
spotting him. As I sat on the bank, a cow moose and her
calf nonchalantly sauntered across the dam wall, poking
holes in it. The beavers, one of them Paddles, immediately set about repairing it.

The moose entered the water, swam to the far shore,
returned twice to persuade her reluctant calf to follow,
which he finally did. When they reached deep water the
youngster laid his head across his mother's neck for
support while they swam. Back on dry land they gave a
healthy shake sending multi-colored droplets into the
sunlit evening.

It was pleasant to sit and watch Paddles and his family
in his natural environment.

A NEW LIFE IN OREGON

Joe and I left Alaska, and moved to Oregon a few days after our daughter's wedding.

We found southern Oregon to be picturesque with an idyllic climate. Our new home sat in a valley surrounded by forests of trees so much bigger than the Black spruce we were used to seeing in Alaska. These trees, were pines, Redwood, Oak, and Blue Spruce. An oak tree over a hundred years old, with branches bigger around than the average Black spruce in Alaska, shaded our front yard.

The mountains were the size of Alaskan foothills, but I knew with time our perspective would change. The weather was gorgeous, temperatures in the sixties, and green lawns everywhere we looked; very different from the snow and cold we left behind.

Building a barn with indoor/outdoor cages for my birds dragged on for weeks. My wholesaler friend said, "No rush," but I wanted the birds with me. Finally, with constructions completed, Joe and I drove to pick them up. He was growing weaker and the long, trip tired him out.

We hoped our children would spend Christmas with us. We missed them horribly; we had never been so far away from them. In the evenings we spent a great deal of time reminiscing about their growing up years. Even on our daily rides to explore Oregon, we chatted about them when some small thing reminded us of time shared when they lived at home.

Joe made appointments with a new doctor, who told me I must make Joe walk every single day. He didn't want to. I drove him anywhere he wanted to go, but insisted he walk to and from the truck down our garden pathway, and to and from a restaurant when we stopped for lunch or coffee. That had to suffice. I refused to spend our time arguing.

Our children made the trip to spend the Christmas holiday season with us. They drove the Alcan Highway. It was to be the last time we'd all be together. Of course, we didn't know that then.

Christmas day dawned bright and sunny. I cooked a traditional dinner, with Janny's and Karis' help. Our house looked as all our Christmas' had: a decorated tree with Janny's first doll at the top. Packages stacked beneath the boughs, plates of cookies, boxes of candy, and stuffed stockings hanging on the wall. Outside the sun sparkled on the pond where George and Weezey, our Black swans, floated like ornaments. That in itself was different from an Alaskan Christmas.

The pond gave Joe and me a great deal of pleasure. Joe built a radio-controlled boat that we both enjoyed, and we loved the wildlife that came to feed and nest. Regular visitors were Mergansers, Coots, Canada Geese and Grebes. The Grebes fascinated me the way they fed their babies feathers for their first food. I learned later, they do it to protect their youngsters against puncture wounds to their stomachs from sharp fish bones. Coots, I had problems with. They attacked their chicks if they persistently begged for food, sometimes killing them. Nature seemed cruel at times. The Canadian geese remained on the pond all winter, and Coyotes stalked the perimeter hoping for an easy meal.

Our children enjoyed the pond during their visits. They hopped into our rowboat and fished for Catfish.

Their visits with us passed all too quickly. The house, too quiet, felt empty without them, but we slipped back into our routine of daily rides. We drove to the coast on old 99, via the Redwood forest. We sat on benches overlooking the beach, watching people and seagulls. The sea air smelled clean, the sun warmed us, and the sound of waves breaking on the shore relaxed us. We ate fresh fish at a small café where locals hung out. Sometimes we drove to the mountains and lunched at Crater Lake Lodge, stopped for a cool drink at Lake of the Woods, or took a short drive down by the Rogue River, where Joe fished while I lazed in the sun with a good book.

One day, Joe and I found a man who sold miniature donkeys. We bought two Jennies. Then we purchased emus, rheas, and sheep to add to our collection. Now we had a mini-farm. Along with operating my bird business, it kept me busy

At night Joe and I companionably sat reading or watching television. I joined a local Bird Club. Joe attended the meetings with me. We made friends, which helped to fill the void left by our children being so far away. We did everything together, with one exception; Joe played poker with a group of men he met on our visits to town. It was good for him to have an interest of his own, and somebody besides me to talk to.

My business kept expanding. I raised and sold hand-fed baby birds to pet stores, some as far away as New York.

Winter turned to spring, and Joe entered the hospital again. At home again a few days later, he assured me, "It's just a matter of time and I'll regain my strength." I believed it because I wanted to.

Every day that summer and fall we tried to see and enjoy as much of Oregon as possible. Between caring for my birds and running my business, the months flew by, and Joe seemed to be a little healthier. As winter approached, we knew it was not going to last.

BACKYARD BATTLE

Every element of my life during the years I lived in Oregon was different from the way I had lived in Alaska. Our home was now ranch style, not daylight basement. My birds lived in indoor/outdoor cages, and I'm sure it felt better to them than being confined to the inside our house. The truck was new, and did not have four-wheel drive. My friends were new. We acquired mini donkeys, emus, black swans, all of which spent the winter outside without my having to worry about them suffering in the cold. The property had an orchard where plums, apples, peaches, grapes, pears, cherries, and nectarines grew.

Around the house, rhododendrons flaunted purple and pink blossoms, and azaleas blazed with orange blooms. Flowers flourished, and a huge weeping willow tree's branches draped over the fence. The wild creatures; birds, orioles, American blue birds, pheasants, quail, and deer that appeared to have no fear of me, visited the shade under a Redwood tree in my yard.

One day, I observed an event I had not seen in Alaska. A pair of swallows nested for the first time in a box I hung on my back porch hoping to temp them. They inspected it for days before it held their final stamp of approval. From then on, every few hours, one or both would return to the box with long, gray feathers molted by my emus, short white ones from my geese. They robbed down from my swan's nest, and I watched them chase and catch various feathers floating on the breeze to line their chosen box in preparation for their future family. Neither I, my cat or my dog seemed to bother them when we sat at our picnic table on the covered porch.

Once their newly furnished home suited them, they mated often on boughs of a nearby tree. The female spent hours inside the box, and I could hear her rearranging the contents to her satisfaction. Then quiet for a whole day. She invited her mate to enter the to-be nursery for his inspection. Apparently please, he left to gather food to bring to her. She poked her head out of the hole to take his offering then returned to laying her eggs and incubating them.

Sometimes the male relieved her long enough to stretch her wings, make several passes over the pond, scooped up insects then return to her motherly duties.

The female sat patiently waiting for the chicks to enter their outside-of-the shell world. The male fed his mate several times a day. After the babies arrived, both parents brought food to them. When the parent returned to the box, the other parent swooped out, collected food then returned. I watched in fascination.

Once the babies had grown big enough to poke their gaping mouths out of the hole, they waited and watched for their parents. When they spotted them, it was a push and shove to fill the hole so only one head could stick out, which left no room for others inside to squeeze through and take the offered food. This continued until they fledged.

The fledgling's first flight was something to behold. One by one they dropped from the box, wildly flapping until their wings looked blurred. Then, making a miraculous recovery, they gained altitude and flew to the nearest tree. All that was under the watchful eyes of their parents.

One day the following spring while I sat watching another pair raise their young, an enemy appeared – a Stella jay, a bird-world villain. With its black talons gripping the edge of the hole in the nesting box, it poked its head inside and fled with a chick tightly clasped in its beak. It happened too fast for me to prevent it. Both parents followed in hot pursuit. A fruitless venture; their youngster was gone. From then on, one parent remained on guard while the other searched for food.

A few days later, another intrusion by the local marauder occurred. This time he took the mother. How bravely her mate fought for her. He dived the jay time and time again, but it was no contest. Then, suddenly, out of the clear blue sky, help arrived. Five other swallows, then more.

The war raged on. Surrounded, the enemy protested loudly while being attacked by tiny dive-bombers to the left and from above. Swarming miniature feathered-spitfires zoomed in from the rear and the right. Angry voices screamed what I thought had to be obscenities as the battle continued over a profusion of petunias. Outnumbered and agitated, the jay dropped its cargo, then sped off beyond the reaches of swallow-territory.

At that point I rushed in to help the wounded mother. I reached down to pick up the open-mouthed, small, quivering body. Frightened, she pecked at my fingers wrapped around her. The male, her lifetime partner, perched on a tree close by observing everything. He was ready to take me on if necessary, it seemed. Meanwhile, the assisting fighter squadron disappeared as quickly as it had arrived.

I talked to the female while checking for damage: two beak punctures, and several pinprick puncture holes from talons. "It's all right. You don't need to be afraid," I told. I walked into the house. Tiny voices emanated from the nest box. Their mother struggled to be free. She pinched a piece of my skin in her beak. "Hang in there, Little one." She quieted and let go.

Inside the house, I separated then removed a few feathers while telling her, "I'm sorry. I know that hurt." Then, carrying her with me, I gathered up hydrogen peroxide and q-tips. Back at the kitchen table. I told her, "This won't take long," as I dabbed antiseptic on her wounds.

A little while later, back on the porch, within earshot of her young's voices, she struggled. I opened my hand to release her. "Go on," I told her. "Go home. Your babies need you." Instead of flying directly to her nest as I had expected, she flew out over the lawn. Her mate winged over and joined her. I eavesdropped on their reunion.

They had fought a valiant battle and won, but with weeks of summer still remaining, I did not believe their war was over.

SLEEPY COMPANIONS

While you're sitting reading this, I'd be willing to bet if you live with a dog or a cat and you sneaked a peek at them, they're napping. I just checked my two companions; they're sleeping.

Not long ago a friend, who was spending a vacation with me said, "Missy's lazy. All she does is sleep, or drift from one place to another to find a place to flop down and nap." My friend was referring to my dog.

Defensively I replied, "She can out distance you any day of the week. She's not lazy. She's content."

Missy, and my cat Cody, are my companions. Cody spends time alone whenever I leave the house. Missy, on the other hand, is alone only on those occasions when the days are too hot or too cold for her to be left in the car.

Over the years, I watched the two of them; in fact, you could say I studied them, and am constantly amazed at the amount of hours they sleep. Cody spends most of her days dozing in her chair, draped over the arm of my recliner, on the bed or in my lap. Missy also wiles away hours in slumber, but I have no doubt she'd work hard and excel if she had a job. I do not believe they are lazy, or that is the reason they sleep.

When Missy arrived on my doorstep, someone had painted her green. I talked to her and she rolled over. It was then I saw brush marks on her hairless stomach. During the hours I worked cleaning her, she patiently lay prone. With such a gentle disposition how could somebody treat her that way?

Cody, I found as a kitten.

Cody, Missy, and I live on a bluff overlooking a Wildlife Refuge. We watch wolves, foxes and coyotes, all hunting voles, hares, and small game in the long grass below my house. Unlike Missy, their lives are busy, filled with hours of searching for food in order to survive. Watching them in action, it is hard to realize that she is a descendant of a wolf. It is that fact which leads me to believe that because I do not expect her to work, provide food or comfortable shelter for herself, I am the main cause of her lazy-appearing lifestyle. Had she been born wild, her days would be filled in the same manner as her ancestors.

Even as she lightly dozes during the day, she is still aware of my every move. Her eyes pop open immediately when she hears the coat closet open. If it's the vacuum I drag out, she barely moves. She closes her eyes in sleep again. When I pull my jacket from its hanger, she is wide-awake, standing and ready to go.

Most days, regardless of the weather, Missy and I take a walk. Always willing to accompany me, it is I who tire, not her. She'd keep going for many more hours than I'm capable of trekking. Not only does she trot along beside me, she races away to investigate everything that moves, and looks or smells interesting. Under the façade of domesticity, she retains her instinct to hunt. At times she chases and catches small critters. Busy with those pursuits she covers several miles.

While I drive, she keeps a watchful eye out for moose along the roadside, woofing if she spots one. When we return to the house, she collapses on her bed and is asleep in seconds, her paws twitching as she chases her dreams. Sometimes she whimpers. I can only hope that it is not due to vague memories of cruelty inflicted upon her in past years.

Missy notifies me when company drives into our yard, chases ravens away when they try to steal her bones, and plays with her buddies when they come to visit. She stalks squirrels that insist on scolding her every time she is outside. She sniffs out her territory for information as to who or what has trespassed. All this she accomplishes in the few hours she is awake.

My acquired knowledge she may never possess. Personally, I don't think she needs it, but harm could befall me without her ability to know what unseen perils lurk beyond my sight and hearing when we're out in the backcountry. With her 220 million olfactory receptors, she is aware of everything in her surroundings. She gains knowledge that rides on a breeze. Having only five to ten million of my own receptors, I depend on her to protect me. My own inadequacies and diminished instincts frustrate me, and I am envious of her capabilities.

Missy has only one habit I object to; she insists on rolling in rotten, dead things, rushing to me for approval, then sitting next to me in the car.

As far as I know, only two things terrorize her. One is thunder, the other earthquakes. I wonder if it's because they have no smell or visible features. When thunder rolls or the ground shakes, she is a quivering, inconsolable eighty-six pound lump, who thinks she is the size of a Pomeranian, and desperately tries to crawl onto my lap.

I believe Missy has no desire to justify her existence or attain goals. She has no deadlines to meet, no appointments to keep. Her time is her own, and she shamelessly sleeps her all-too-short life away.

Unlike Cody, who was unconcerned with such things, Missy's nature is to please. Her attributes are many. She forgives without reservation, is unconditionally faithful, never appears restless, and she holds no grudges. She is content with the amount of attention she receives. In return for all she contributes to my life, she expects nothing, but appreciates everything; her foam-padded bed, ample food, a kind voice, a gentle pat, and my company. And, unlike me, she is able to sleep anywhere, any time, guilt free.

MY BLACK SWANS

In my field just to the right of my back door in Oregon, where I lived for fourteen years, are two ponds located a short distance from each other. A year-round creek gently flows through them both. Wild Canadian Honkers, Mergansers, Wood Ducks and, of course, Mallards visited daily. Mallards, it seems, appear anywhere there is a puddle large enough to paddle in. The Wood Ducks nested in two boxes I set up for them; one on a Willow tree, the other on a post. After their eggs hatched and the babies bounced to earth, they immediately followed their mother to one of the ponds. Then Merganser pairs took over the nests boxes.

My Black Swans, native to Australia, lived on one pond. Not compatible with my other swans, a pair of young Black Necks, native to South America, lived inside a fenced area surrounding the other pond. Each pond had an island where the birds nested. My Black Swans built a very large nest constructed of twigs, sticks, feathers, and any other suitable material they found.

The mating ritual of my Black Swans, George and Weezey, I compared to water ballet. Facing each other, they bowed their heads and necks while their bodies undulated in the water. Circling together, they dipped and wrapped necks. When Weezey was sufficiently woed, she stretches her neck out under water and lowered herself until her back was level with the surface. George mounted her, holding her neck feathers in his beak. At that point, only Weezey's head showed above water. When the mating was completed both swans "stood" on the water, flapping full-spread wings, "talking" to each other.

When their eggs hatched, both parents were protective and caring of their brood. Every year, George had one special baby that was a constant companion. While Weezey allowed all the babies to catch a ride on her back, George allowed only his tiny, privileged fluff ball youngster.

When George had gained adulthood, he flew. Most of the time he stayed within hearing distance of Weezey's calls, but at two years of age he flew to the Rogue River, approximately ten road miles from his home, leaving a grieving Weezey, to pace and call for his return.

Notified he was seen in the company of a large flock of domestic geese and ducks, and knowing his exact location, I arrived at the river, a loaf of bread in hand. He swam straight to me. I grabbed him and took him home. Weezey, delighted to see and hear him, ran to him with all the loving greetings she could muster. Eager to reunite them, I neglected to clip his wings before he rushed away. Later, I found it to be a bad mistake. They hurried to their pond in anticipation of mating.

The following year, off to the river George flew again. We went through the same procedure as the year before. Once more, Weezey was ecstatic to see him upon his return. That time I remembered to clip his wing feathers.

The third year he disappeared for five weeks. I searched the river daily, finding no signs of him. Then one day late in the summer, all dressed up in white skirt, white blouse, and white high-heeled shoes to go to town, I saw him in the middle of the same flock of geese and ducks he'd been with the previously.

After parking my truck, I walked to the river's edge. When I called him, he swam over to me, but not close enough for me to grab him. Telling him I'd be back with bread and to wait for me, I left. He waited. I threw bread to tempt him. Immediately, I was surrounded by dozens of geese and ducks. George stood on the outer edge of the hungry mass milling at my feet.

Two loaves of bread later, I thought he was close enough to reach. Lunging forward, I grabbed for him. I missed. He ran. A crowd of people gathered to watch. I raced to stop his escape into the river, falling face down in the process. So much for my white summer outfit! The ground was smothered in goopy, slimy, slippery duck and goose droppings. By now my disposition was in the same disarray as my clothing.

I plunged into the water, swam after George, grabbed him by the neck then headed for the shore. He struggled and beat me with his powerful wings. Bedraggled, embarrassed, disgruntled and shoeless, I picked him up and walked to the

171

truck. People cheered and laughed. A man wandered over and asked, "Your swan?"

I drove home, clipped George's wings to nubs then turned him loose. He ran to Weezey. She turned her beak into the air and walked away from him. He apparently had done that once too often! It was three weeks before she even acknowledged his existence.

A year later I kept a female from the clutch of babies. George allowed her to remain part of his family. A male he would not have tolerated. True to her name, "Auntie" she helped care for the new babies. At times, George and his new little pet of the year wandered into the field, leaving Auntie and Weezey to protect the other youngsters on the pond. Before "Auntie," he never left Weezey alone with their cygnets. I can only assume he had great faith in Auntie.

George and Weezey lived with me for eleven years. They came to me as little puffs of light gray fluff. For eight of those years they produced their own fluff ball babies, usually six to a clutch. Why George had been errant in his ways as an immature swan I can only guess. Maybe it was because he and Weezey did not bond enough for total commitment until they produced young.

HOME AGAIN

After living in Alaska for more than two decades, in 1984, circumstances dictated my husband and I move. We settled in Oregon, and learned to love its predictable seasons. We rafted rivers, picnicked beside picturesque lakes, and walked among thousand-year-old Redwoods. In wintertime, we drove Old 99 to the coast, where we sat in warm sunshine watching waves crash against a rocky shoreline or gently lapping upon miles of flawless sand. Before returning to our mini-ranch in the small, town of Rogue River, we dined on fish caught that morning, in a restaurant overlooking a small-boat harbor.

During those years I never gave up hope of returning to the land that refused to release its hold on my heart. Every year, the minute I stepped from the plane in Anchorage, on my Christmas visits to my children after my husband passed away, I felt like I was home.

Then, in 1997 a friend and I drove to Alaska, via the Cassiar Highway, to spend a summer vacation with my children, who all lived in the state. That trip changed my life. I bought a house built on an eighty-foot bluff overlooking a 28,000 thousand-acre game refuge with an unobstructed view of the Chugach Mountains; it was exactly what I pictured during my absence. Then, after spending four weeks enjoying my family and exploring the state, my friend and I returned to Oregon. The following year I sold my house there and moved to my new home outside Wasilla.

Now, I sit in my living room to watch the sun rise behind silhouetted snow-tipped peaks that bathe the valley below in a golden glow. The light exposes moose; their antlers tipped in amber, browsing on brush, and Sandhill cranes, the color of wet sand, searching for frogs in swampy ground. On a lake, two pairs of swans, glistening white, float amid lily pads. Some days I gaze through a curtain of fog like steam on a bathroom mirror, as sunrays spear through mist clinging to the mountain slopes then pierce their way to the valley floor.

Evening sunsets paint the mountains orange, fuchsia-pink, and then purple. Darkness follows the same path where, that morning, sunlight had banished shadows. Later, the moon creeps from behind Pioneer Peak and craggy Twin Peaks to illuminate the valley in pearl-light, and creatures of the night venture out.

On clear winter nights, Northern Lights, cranberry red, pastel pink, lettuce green, and vanilla ice cream colored strands dance their colorful way across infinity. Stars, like jewels, glistens behind the multihued veil.

As weather permits, daytime walks are a favorite pastime for my dog, Missy, and me. There are special areas we enjoy. One of those is where a beaver family lives. Their lodge, a large mound of mud and sticks, protrudes well above the surface in the middle of their pond.

In summer, the small lake the beaver family created reflects blue skies or gray threatening clouds. In fall, multitudes of wild ducks and geese gather there to prepare for their departure to warmer climes. Frozen over in winter, it's where I search for wild animal tracks: fox, coyote, ptarmigan, and hare. The icebound pond is also where ravens scavenge fish remains left behind by hardy souls who brave the cold.

Springtime brings mosquitoes. They infest the mossy ground surrounding the pond. They rise in clouds with each step Missy and I take. I hear woodpeckers drilling tree trunks, seeking bugs, or watch an eagle that looks like a painting as it perches on a dead limb. Missy spots the beavers with their young, and Pintails, Widgeons, Mergansers, and Mallards that brought their newly hatched babies for their first excursion. In her excitement, she leaps into the water, but finds it colder than expected. She makes a hasty retreat back to the bank. We sit side by side and watch minnows swimming through sunrays down to shadowed water, where they hide close to the bank.

I watch ravens performing their mating rituals and playing aerial games. Hawks hover, looking for voles scampering among scrubby undergrowth far below them. Ever watchful for any prey, eagles soar higher in the sky.

During the summer, swallows dive after newly hatched mosquitoes swarming above the water. Red Poll finches with dull poppy-red crowns, and flocks of waxwings crowd nearby trees. Pine Grosbeaks and Black-capped Chickadees search for a place amid evergreens, out of the sun. Sandhill cranes musical calls fill the air as they circle above us.

When fall arrives, snow-capped mountains, piercing a poker-chip-blue sky, frame the Matanuska valley. It is a time of long shadows and chilly days. The air hangs crisp and clear over foothills covered in deep orange and flaming reds. Flowering fuchsia-colored fireweeds accent trees waiting to drop their foliage in the last days of September. Variegated yellow colored leaves like golden butterflies drift earthward.

In winter, I bundle up in all the clothes I can pile on, and Missy, seemingly oblivious to the freezing temperature, accompanies me on a trek to the beaver pond. Unaware of the beauty I see, she bounds through knee-deep snow. She races out of sight. Later she returns, drops a soggy but unhurt vole at my feet. Hoping it survives I place the tiny creature in dry spruce needles under a tree.

On our hike back to the car, the landscape of sun, shadows, and feathery lace enchant me. As though wrapped in perfectly cut jewels, frost-festooned twigs glisten.

After a day outside, it's pleasant to be back in my house, with hands wrapped around a mug of hot chocolate, sitting in front of a fire, watching flames dancing, listening to logs popping, and seeing Missy sprawled out on the floor warming her tummy while dreaming doggy dreams. It's peaceful, relaxing, and gives me time to reminisce about how the tapestry changes with the weather. Once again I remind myself of the feelings I have for this place I can call home once more.

BIOGRAPHY

Avril Johannes was born and raised in England. She moved to Alaska in 1996. A professional Aviculturist for thirty-four years, she has published short stories in *Reader's Digest*, *Bird Breeder*, *Alaska Magazine*, and various anthologies.

With her daughter, Jan Branham, she has co-authored three children's book; *Squeak, An Alaskan Squirrel, Eeny, Meeny, Miney, Moe, Four Alaskan Ravens*, and *Bunny, An Alaskan Hare*. Her novel, *When The Wolf Calls*, is available in bookstores. *Far North Tales* is a collection of short stories about life with her family.